1-31-72

A HOUSE FOR HOPE
A STUDY IN PROCESS
AND BIBLICAL THOUGHT

Books by WILLIAM A. BEARDSLEE
Published by THE WESTMINSTER PRESS

A House for Hope:
A Study in Process and Biblical Thought

America and the Future of Theology (Ed.)

A House for Hope

A STUDY IN PROCESS AND BIBLICAL THOUGHT

by William A. Beardslee

THE WESTMINSTER PRESS
Philadelphia

ISBN 0-664-20931-9

LIBRARY OF CONGRESS CATALOG CARD No. 75-181724

PUBLISHED BY THE WESTMINSTER PRESS®
PHILADELPHIA, PENNSYLVANIA

PRINTED IN THE UNITED STATES OF AMERICA

*For Kit
Companion in the Pilgrimage
of Hope*

Contents

Introduction

This book is about simple things—about hope, which makes love more than a thing of the moment, and about faith, which gives us a horizon within which we can trust ourselves to love and hope. It is a mark of wisdom to speak simply about great simple realities such as faith, hope, and love.

But it is not always easy or even possible to speak as simply as we long to do. We can speak simply only when things come clear. Sometimes they stubbornly refuse to come clear, and those are times of confusion. In such a time of confusion we find ourselves today. It is a time when it is painfully difficult to speak simply without being trite or false.

When we are in a difficulty we can never be sure of the way out in advance. But we must try to gain a new perspective on the simple things that have become so hard to speak about. To do that we shall have to give up speaking as simply as we should like to do, because we are struggling with what we do not quite know as yet. That is the only route to a new vision in which we may speak simply once more.

This book explores what hope can be in a perspective that draws on both modern process philosophy and the insights and way of life known in Christian faith. It is very much a book written from Christian conviction, from the belief that the insights hammered out in the centuries of Judeo-Christian existence are still the profoundest center in which to stand in order to find what it is to be human, or to put it differently, in the belief that the experience of the Judeo-Christian tradition is experience of reality. But the book is also written from the conviction that no part of the Christian interpretation of faith can be free from question, change, or even rejection. For whether we like it or not, we must live in the world as men experience it today. It is surely legitimate to claim that faith runs counter to the prevailing trend of the culture! It is also legitimate to hold provisionally an intellectual position that runs counter to what is accepted as true in our culture. But faith is always formed by culture even when it is criticizing it, and the healthy interaction between faith and culture requires that we constantly rethink our faith in terms of the rest of our understanding of reality. To keep faith and culture in separate compartments can be justified only as a temporary measure, until further clarification of how they both speak of the same reality is possible. If it is not possible, faith will be forced into a separate world of its own.

Today much of the most exciting theology is about hope and the future. But too often it does not examine itself very thoroughly in the terms set forth here, because it takes its starting point in faith too much for granted. In most of this book I shall not be discussing the well-known theologians of hope and the future. I am grateful to them, and I have learned much more from them than is set forth in this book. But what I have tried to do here is to follow a different path, and to explore the meaning of hope in "the future as process."

The plan of the book is to begin with the most general and universally human basis of hope, which is found in the biology of sex and growth, then to work step by step toward the central Christian confession—our trust in the figure of Christ as a focus of hope. The plan is to move from nature to grace, from sex and human creativeness to man's struggle with the infinite God, and from there to the distinctively Christian themes of secularization and eschatology, or hope for the end, to speak only at the last about what Christ can mean for hope in the future as process. To do this is to go at it backward, from the point of view of those who say that Christ is the point at which Christian thinking must begin.

I do not care to argue the merits of the other way of doing theology by beginning with Christ. The way chosen here has the advantage of making clear step by step how the new vision of the world which the process thinking of Alfred North Whitehead and his followers can give us affords a new angle of vision on hope. In a world newly seen from this perspective, the Christian style of hope is reshaped, but it still remains—I believe—Christian hope. Whitehead's philosophy gives us a chance to see how the world and faith belong together, in a way that most other ways of thinking about Christian faith find hard to do. I have tried to keep the technical vocabulary of Whitehead's thought to a minimum, for he set forth his ideas in a very difficult language. What is necessary has been brought in, however, in each chapter bit by bit as the discussion moves its way from the most general human experiences to the specifically Christian historical stance and to the meaning of Christ. (Readers who wish first to orient themselves to the thought and vocabulary of Alfred North Whitehead may, before reading the chapters that follow, turn to the Appendix: A Note on Whitehead's Terminology, at the end of the book; others will prefer to read right on and turn to it only as needed.) I hope that it is clear to the reader from the start that Whitehead's philosophy is not itself Christian and does not establish the validity of Christian hope. I hope as well that it will become clear that this perspective does give us a vision in which many aspects of Christian hope open up as possibilities more clearly than they do from other points of view.

Of course Christian insights will be changed as they are, so to speak, seen through a new prism. The reader will find that such basic components of the Christian tradition as the commandment to "have no other gods before me" and the doctrine of the Trinity are questioned and broken down, but in an effort to draw out a view in which the intention of the Christian insight will come to a fuller expression.

Hope is terribly problematic today, even though it has always been central to Christian faith. How deeply faith is part of its world is shown by the fact that where we find powerful hope and joy in Christianity, they come to expression by breaking with form and tradition, as in the moving work of Corita Kent. Hope seems to be of the moment. But this can be only half the story. Hope cannot live only in the moment. It needs a "house," a place where it is at home. I believe that the framework of the future as process best helps us today to see where the home or house of hope is. In a group of young artists and actors, I was asked what I was working on. I said that I was writing on "the structure of hope," for that was the title I had taken then for this book. Quickly enough we were in a brisk argument, for it seemed to them that "structure" and "hope" did not belong together. They put hope and spontaneity together, and any kind of structure that set a framework for hope seemed repressive. The evening's discussion was extremely enlightening to me, and I have learned a lot from it. Spontaneity is of the essence of hope, and far more deeply so than our traditional religion has recognized. But the rejection of structure is destructive of hope. In rebellion against outmoded and rigid structure, we may feel that hope can live only with pure spontaneity. But spontaneity and freedom require a setting, even when they struggle against it. The setting of process thinking, which takes both freedom and structure seriously, can show us how hope can live amid the uncertainties and in the truly open situation in which we are.

No one can speak to the uncertainties of today who does not share them. From that fact some draw the conclusion that the only authentic modern voice is the voice of uncertainty or even of despair. The journey in quest of hope offered in the following chapters has not been undertaken from a position of detachment or of security. Nor has it been written because I am personally of a particularly hopeful temperament. It has been written from the profound conviction that there are powers of hope in our heritage which are still viable, and the voice that will uncover the true resources for the future must speak not just from the immediate experience of uncertainty or loss of meaning, but must struggle to see anew, in a modern framework, what has opened men to the future in previous times. We must speak of Christ not only in terms of suffering and death but also of life and joy. May it be that this is the way!

Acknowledgments

Most of this book was written at the School of Theology at Claremont during a year of sabbatical leave and a subsequent summer. I wish to express my gratitude for the warm reception that I was given there and for the facilitation of my project in particular by the staff of the library. My work has been stimulated especially by my long association with a vigorous group of thinkers at Emory University (including at one time Charles Hartshorne) as well as by lively interchange with many at Claremont. My particular thanks are due to John B. Cobb, Jr., whose careful comment has both clarified and challenged my thinking in countless ways. The Ossabaw Island Project provided a brief but much needed period for uninterrupted writing. I am indebted to the Emory University Research Committee for assistance and to Pomona College for a fruitful semester as Visiting Professor. Most of Chapter V appeared in the *Journal of the American Academy of Religion*, Vol. XXXVIII, No. 3 (September, 1970), pp. 227-239, and is reprinted by permission. Most of Chapter VI appeared in *Transitions in Biblical Scholarship*, ed. by J. Coert Rylaarsdam (The University of Chicago Press, 1968; © 1968 by The University of Chicago Press), and is reprinted by permission of the publishers.

W. A. B.

Part One
HOPE AND GOD

I

Sex

BIOLOGICAL BASES FOR HOPE:
GROWTH AND REPRODUCTION

A woman living in an urban ghetto is asked by a reporter what hope she has, living as she must. She points to her children: "They are my hope," she says. This simple episode shows how profoundly mysterious hope is, how it is often present in the most discouraging of circumstances, though it often evaporates when times are easier. The episode also shows how deeply rooted hope is in the biology of reproduction. The child is the fundamental focus of hope and, more broadly, the paradigm of hope. This point is important to make, since at first sight, hope may seem to be more dimly related to our biological nature than almost any other mental-emotional response. The style of interpretation that emphasizes man's closeness to his biological roots usually downplays hope. In the theological sphere this latter stance is impressively and consistently developed by Richard L. Rubenstein, who combines a sensitive Freudianism with a deep appreciation for the archaic or pagan elements in Judaism, and who explicitly holds that the directional, hope-oriented aspect of Judaism and Christianity is without basis.

" 'Eschatology is a sickness.' . . . It was our Jewish sickness originally. We gave it to you [Christians]. You took us seriously. Would that you hadn't! . . . If you are a Christian, you cannot avoid it. If you become post-Christian, choose pagan hopelessness rather than the false illusion of apocalyptic hope." [1]

In the face of the widespread mood of rejecting hope and of establishing a more "realistic" and less idealistic view of man by rediscovering his body, it is important to see that hope does have inescapable biological roots. These will not prove that hope has an inevitable or rightful place in human existence. But to see them clearly and to clarify the physical rootage of hope will not only balance a prevalent one-sided interpretation of man's bodily nature, but will help us to see the depth in which the self-transcendence of hope is based.

The biological basis of hope can be taken to be the directionality of biological growth or the directionality of sexual reproduction. There is much to be said for taking the former alternative, growth, as the biological perspective from which to understand hope. Then growth can be understood as an "open" side of self-preservation; starting this way, hope is openly and unashamedly hope for oneself. Such an approach helps us to understand how hope is a characteristically youthful property—the potential of growth is associated with the young self's reaching forward to the future in hope. This way of approaching hope would not only illuminate some of the connections between hope and creativity, but would tie in with the easily observed fact that hope is most obviously a property of children. The children of the American urban ghetto or of an Asian metropolis show the unfolding of hope as readily as do the children of the economically privileged, as anyone knows who has been among them. As the inexorable closing-off of opportunities takes place, as growth reaches its term, hope contracts. The horizon of hope closes with the passage of time, and the hopelessness of age replaces the hopefulness of youth.

Such a perspective has the merit of making contact with psychological studies that indicate the healthfulness or wholeness of the self which is open to growth; at least under certain circumstances the hopefulness of youth does not have to be abandoned in maturity. Hope may still be meaningful in terms of realistic growth and openness to new possibilities. Important work by psychologists shows the fruitfulness of this approach.[2] Furthermore, hope as an expression of the self's readiness to respond openly to the next moment can be related to a basic religious insight that the utter core of faith is the stance of receiving the next moment as a gift. An interpretation of hope connecting man's basic biological tendency to preserve himself, his openness to biological and cultural growth, and his religious stance of receptivity to the gift of the next moment of existence can create an avenue to an impressive recovery of hope.

The Child as the Focus of Hope

Nevertheless, we propose a different biological function as a paradigm to clarify the nature of hope. It can be simply put:

> To have a child is to hope,
> And to hope is to have a child.

The most illuminating biological basis for hope is sex. The peculiar drive and texture of human hope arise in part, it is true, from the tendency for self-preservation modified toward the growth of a new self. But sex as the process by which the line of life is projected forward through time is the best key to hope. Hope for the child is the most persistent form of hope, and in fact the only concrete form of hope available to the greater part of humanity under the terrible economic pressures that have been the lot of most men, as is dramatically shown by such a book as that by James Agee and Walker Evans, *Let Us Now Praise Famous Men*.[3] So far as we can penetrate animal existence, the nearest analogue to human hope that we see there is the care of animals for their young. In that phase of animal existence in many forms of life, there is an intense channeling of energy into the protection and nurture of the young life—anthropomorphically speaking, a self-denial for the sake of the coming reality—that is well known to all who have observed the life, for instance, of mammals or birds. The willingness to forgo immediate satisfaction for the sake of a coming reality is a basic mark of all hope, and this aspect of hope is most decisively expressed on the biological level in the parent-child relationship, which in so many of the more complex forms of life functions unconsciously in this very pattern of deferring immediate satisfaction for the sake of the child.

THE GAP BETWEEN THE TWO PHASES OF SEX

Thus we come to a striking feature of sex—one highlighted by the way in which it functions in our culture—namely, the separation between its immediate phase of sexual union and its long-term consequence of offspring. Animals, and it is said certain archaic tribes, have no consciousness of the connection between the two phases. These two phases, inexorably built together by biological fact but separable in experience, have to be welded together by some cultural structure. The family, varied as its forms are in different cultures, functions in all of them to hold together the two phases of sex, so that the care of children is the consequence of sexual union. In our own culture, probably partly as a reaction against a period of strong emphasis on a close connection between the two phases, sexual union and the care and hope for children are now tending to fall apart. This trend hardly needs to be documented, and it is interestingly shown in the use of language: having children is hardly a sexual act, as we use the term "sex."

Our culture means by sex the first phase of biological sex, sexual union. The celebrations of sex in the American arts from advertising to writing, the film, and the theater have almost entirely to do with this phase of sex. The separation of the immediately erotic from the rigidities of the traditional family structure has been widely hailed as liberating and hopeful. This trend is understandable as a reaction against the cultural suppression of much of the freedom, beauty, and excitement of the erotic. No doubt it has been immensely aided by the technological developments summarized under the term "the pill," though it should not be forgotten that techniques of contraception and abortion have been known and practiced for centuries. It seems that this trend toward separating sex and children has been even more basically furthered by the general affluence of so much of the area of the world dominated by Western culture. An offhand first response to those who see the separation of the two phases of sex as hopeful would therefore be to see how sex and affluence have worked together in other cultures. A reading of the Roman satirists and historians should be a sobering experience in this connection.

That is only a first response to a very complex change. It is not intended as a polemic against the recognition of ourselves as deeply constituted by our bodily sexuality, nor as a denial of the profound insights of Freud into the immense influence of the unconscious on our behavior and into the large sexual component of the unconscious. In point of fact, the very Puritan heritage that is so widely blamed for its repressiveness of sex was one of the channels through which an appreciation of sex, and even of its playful aspect, was brought to expression in our culture. The Puritan rejected the ascetic ideal of celibacy and emphasized the healthfulness of the sexual side of marriage. The modern sex manual has its literary ancestor in the frank Puritan marriage sermon.[4] But more than this: sexual union affords a direct if often mute avenue toward awareness of the sacred. A remark attributed to a modern theologian is puzzling: He who longs for the infinite while in his beloved's arms is guilty of bad taste. One would think it more natural to ask, What else would he be longing for at such a time? Instead of opposing the association of sex and the sacred, I would affirm sexual union as a fundamental access to the mystery of existence.[5]

The current emphasis on the immediacy, the freedom, and the longing for totality that sex as union symbolizes is highlighted by the particular cultural situation in which we find ourselves, a situation in which freedom is emotionally associated with aversion from long-term goals. But the direction of this symbolization is built into the delight and intensity of the sexual encounter itself. It is of the moment, not of the future. The liberation of sexuality in our culture is profoundly connected with a rejection of long-term satisfactions. But the second pole of sex—the birth of children—is just as profoundly connected with a long-term process moving into the future. Love as erotic union expresses a longing for totality which becomes a longing for death. The affiliation between erotic love as a longing for totality and the desire for death as also a longing for totality is made clearer when erotic sex is detached from the life and future-oriented consequence of children. Thus the medieval courtly lover, whose love was in principle outside the family, had the connection between love and death explicitly drawn out for him in the poetry of courtly love.[6] Until not long ago the modern imagination, by drawing erotic love back into marriage and thus bringing to expression its movement beyond the moment into the future, has concealed the affinity between erotic love and death. But in still more recent times the connection between love and death has again become evident, and with a force and violence that the medieval mythical structure was able to channel and control. Many of the perplexities of our time with sex can be illuminated from this point of view: the rigidities of marriage were rejected as not life-giving, but the intensity and passion that were sought outside of the traditional relationship did not prove to be life-giving either. Erotic love is biologically life-giving only in terms of the next generation, and if this connection is canceled out, the intensity of love, its thirst for totality, soon discloses its affinity with the longing for the totality of death.

It is true that the affinity between total intensity and death does not come out so clearly when biological growth is taken as the basic biological model. Then the tensions between the intensity of immediate satisfaction and the achievement of long-term goals can be seen as manageable, and the moments of intensity, including sexual intensity, can be seen as finding their place within a life of growth which accepts the fact that death is the terminus of growth. Such a pattern lies behind some of the most penetrating psychological interpretations of the structure of existence. But it is noteworthy that such interpretations usually do not make much either of the procreative function of sex or of hope as a fundamental human stance. Thus Abraham Maslow's important book *Toward a Psychology of Being,*[7] sets up a model of cognition that contrasts "deficiency-cognition" with "being-cognition." In this model, deficiency-cognition is oriented toward the future as the focus of active striving, or of self-projection, but being-cognition is disoriented to time, and is a perception of a pure present. Maslow's study of "self-actualizing" individuals and of "peak experiences" is extremely fruitful in dispelling the notion that the overcoming of deficiency is the fundamental energy of the self. His emphases on growth through delight and on the future as dynamically active in the present are important for an understanding of hope. Further, he has shown that peak experiences are not simply momentary but have profound aftereffects. But his strong emphasis on the way in which peak experiences are sufficient unto themselves leads us to inquire whether Maslow has overlooked other, more future-oriented experiences, which disclose linkage toward the future.

Maslow does not find empirical data which would lead him to modify his model to include a forward-looking hope that is transformed into something more than self-actualization, and it may be that he has not found these data because hope for the future is eroded in our culture. But more important is the fact that hope does not readily express itself in a moment of detachment, illumination, and totality such as that expressed in ecstasy including the ecstasy of erotic sex. Maslow's data, like the important work of Marghanita Laski on ecstasy,[8] are gathered from reports of moments of psychic intensity, and both Maslow's and Laski's materials emphasize the aspects of disorientation, timelessness, and detachment of the peak experience or ecstasy. Such cherished moments are obviously of immense human significance. The preoccupation with sex in our culture and the pursuit of ecstasy through the deserts of desacralized sexual experience testify to a longing for this moment of totality even when it cannot be found. But this line of investigation will remain opaque to the search for the phenomenon of hope, since hope and disorientation to time do not belong together. Ernst Bloch has pointed to a different type of psychological experience as the field in which to explore hope —the daydream, in which the ego (with its orientation to time) remains dominant in the imagination, even though "reality" is transformed into the dreamed-of world.[9]

We shall have to return to these two styles of pointing toward "perfection," the style of loss of self in totality, and the style of projection of self forward into an open future. For the moment, however, we return to the biological level, to point out (what is obvious) that biologically the whole point of the moment of erotic intensity is that something comes out of it; through it the energies of life are projected into the future. The second phase of sex, biologically just as "sexual" as the first—the coming of the child—orients the parents toward the future rather than toward the moment. In this phase the relationship of caring for the other cannot remain the closed totality that it proclaims itself to be in the moments of making love. From the biological point of view, this second phase is what sex is there for. In a sense, therefore, our culture's use of sex is a Promethean effort to liberate one phase of sex from its total biological meaning.

From this point of view, the reactionary pronouncements of the papacy about birth control gain a different perspective from that in which the thoughtful modern viewer usually first sees them. The traditional Roman Catholic view has the wis-

dom of the continuing effort of culture not to put asunder
what biology has joined together. The family is the traditional
means of effecting the union of erotic concern for the moment
and child-oriented concern for the future. But the particular
way in which the two phases of sex are held together in the
papal position will not find wide support. Social and technological changes have made the traditional Roman Catholic opposition to birth control no longer tenable—as indeed is
widely recognized by urbanized Catholics. However, it is
important to note that while one thrust of criticism of this traditional position faults it for its downgrading of what we have
called the first phase of sex, the clinching pragmatic argument
against it comes from its failure to do justice to the real requirements of the second phase. For the papal position completely fails to come to grips with the conflict between the
"natural" consequence of the production of children and the
social consequence of the population explosion. That is, the
traditional view has to be rejected primarily because it ob-
structs care for the child.

But all this should not lead one to overlook one of the basic
intentions behind this rigid and unacceptable position. The
claim of the future, the child, is fundamentally more important in sex than the claim of the longing for total presence, for
ecstasy in the moment. The trouble with the papal position is
not that it affirms this, but that it affirms it unintelligently
and in a way that chokes off the fundamental meaning of hope
that is expressed in the relationship to the child. It is true,
however, that the task of finding an adequate way, functional
in terms of our present knowledge, by which the fundamental
biological connection between the present and future in sex
and the family can be expressed is enormously difficult. Despite all the freedoms that modern knowledge gives men,
there is little reason to think that we are at the point of being
liberated from the basic structure of concern for the future
that the traditional view expresses. The view of our biological
nature that we find so widely expressed today is a singularly

one-sided one. Biological sex taken as a whole expresses openness to the future in its total rhythm, and not just in the intensity of the moment—an openness to the future of which the child is the biological symbol and the biological reality.

For our purposes, it is not important to settle the question how far we can liberate human life from its original biological patterns, or to decide what the consequences of such liberation will be. On the one hand, social changes in the role of women will mean that the child will be (and indeed has already been) increasingly recognized as the concern of both parents. On the other hand, the threats to ecological balance may bring about a strongly conservative attitude toward biological and technological innovation. But in spite of this possible and well-grounded reaction, the discoveries which are now being made will bring us into a period of hitherto unsuspected "biological freedom," freedom to reshape the mechanisms of heredity and reproduction as well as many other biological processes, to an extent that would have seemed fantastic only a few years ago. For better or worse, we shall enter this realm of experimentation. Technical considerations —what can actually be done—will determine many of the results. But fundamentally the results will be shaped by our aims, by what we intend. We will be changed in unexpected ways by biological technology, but we need not be its slaves, even though many of the changes will be irreversible. If our aims are to be wise, they must take account of the whole meaning of the processes upon which we exercise our freedom.

The manipulative freedom of modern science and technology has tended to reinforce the focus of consciousness on sexual union as the meaning of sex, while those who have had a grasp of the need for some social cement to hold the two phases together have often appeared to be repressive reactionaries with no grasp of biological reality. We are not appealing here for a traditional solution to any of the problems raised by biological experimentation, but are pointing to the necessity of keeping the functional meaning of both phases of sex in view as we grapple with the new issues. The biological root of hope in sex as procreation, the transcendence of the moment which comes as one is taken beyond himself into the next generation—this is the basis of hope's persistence in the face of hopeless situations as well as the root of hope's willingness to defer immediate satisfaction. That the specific forms which express this biological hope vary from society to society must not obscure the fact that this claim of the future is as "bodily" and as deeply rooted in our nature as is the more immediate satisfaction of sexual union.

THE PROBLEM OF WASTE

At the same time, the connection between biological processes and human hope is a painful one, most evidently because the biology of reproduction involves a fantastic amount of "waste." The animal may devote an immense portion of its energy to taking care of its young, but most of the young cannot survive for long. If young birds are taken from the nest by a cat or a snake, the parents return to the nest for a day or so, but very soon the biological signal that directs them to do this is turned off; if it is early enough in the season, another signal soon directs them to mate and raise another brood. So short is human memory that it will be hard for many of the readers of this book to realize that the conditions of human family life, for most of the world's population, function in a pattern very similar to this, or did so until a generation or two ago. Through the years it has been the way things work that a large family was born, of whom in most cases few survived. But this "waste," this harsh pattern, did not close off hope. Indeed, it is of the essence of hope that it does not always have to be satisfied. The basic biological-social unit of the family is so illuminating as a model for hope not only because it juxtaposes hope, precariousness, and waste, but because it brings to light more decisively than the alternate biological model of growth can do the element of self-denial for the sake of the future which is in a strange way also a projection of one's self.

HOPE AND THE CONFLICT BETWEEN PARENT AND CHILD

There will be those who will object that our model for hope is based on an unreasonably simple or even sentimental view of the relationship between parent and child. The child is also a symbol of death to the parent, and the parent is a symbol of death to the child. We know this all too well today, and we are indebted to Freud for bringing into the open aspects of the meaning of the child which we do not readily recognize. Freud's view that religion originated in the murder of the father by the "primal horde" in order that they might get possession of the father's females is not taken seriously by historians of religion as a description of how religion actually arose. But that does not lessen the significance of this vision of conflict at the core of the relation between father and son.[10] The relevance of this Freudian insight for the question of hope is that it points to the problematic of hope, that hope is dependent upon a future beyond ourselves, and in some sense implies an effort to control the future. But the future may resist control, may take the power and direction of life into its own hands. The most hopeful parent may be the most tyrannical, and may from the child's point of view be thrusting him toward death and not life, whereas the vitality of the younger generation appears as a death-dealing threat to their elders, as we can so plainly see from the headlines we read in the last third of this century.

The mutual desire for the other's death is real enough in the relation between parent and child, and the fact that this competitive desire has been so largely papered over by social control, repressed, and then discovered in the unconscious has given many interpreters of modern life the feeling that by getting at this aspect of the relationship, they were getting at the "real" relationship, whereas the older sustaining and transmissive model was a social fiction. But a balanced view will see it the other way around. The child is a threat because he is an object of hope: the child as hope is primary, and without that meaning, the whole structure of conflict which Freud analyzed would be without profound significance.

Further, the turmoil in the relation between the generations so evident in our culture does not undermine the fundamental structure of hope that moves from generation to generation. The conflict between the young and the old is a sign of readjustment in their relationship, and it is the fruit above all of the extended period of preadult existence which a complex technological society has forced upon young people. The older generation has extended the notion of the child beyond the age in which it is appropriate, and the younger generation is rejecting the style of adult life prepared for it by its elders, but these facts do not destroy the meaning of the new generation as the focus of hope. The point is that hope, with its pattern of anticipation, movement toward and waiting for a goal, and deferment of immediate satisfaction in favor of a creativity that will be operative in the future, is as deeply rooted in our biological nature as is the more accentuated stance of intensity or ecstasy, in which the present moment is "all." This is a simple enough point, but it is worth stressing, since it is so often said that the second stance, the stance of immediacy, is more "natural," and the stance of hope, waiting, and intentionality is imposed on human nature by culture. Human biological nature does not provide an organized specific relationship between the two stances, as animal life does, but nonetheless no distinction between the one stance as natural and the other as imposed can be made. Both stances have deep physical roots; each finds its most powerful biological expression in one of the two phases of sex—and both are shaped by culture, for human nature apart from culture is an abstraction. That the two elements are often in tension with each other has nothing to do with the supposed secondary or imposed nature of restraints on immediacy and intensity of experience.

On the contrary, as far as a purely biological view of man's nature is concerned, one would have to say that deferment and hope express a more fundamental biological reality than immediate intensity does, for the child is the fundamental and functional reason for the intensity of sexual encounter. It is not my purpose to suggest that people enjoy sex because they expect to have children! The point is that the retrospective view, which can be aware of and appreciate both phases of sex, and can therefore be future-oriented, is more revealing than the awareness of the moment. It is one of the oddities of our supposedly knowledgeable age that we restrict the word "sex" to only one part, and in the long run the less central part, of its meaning. This narrowness of vision expresses a longing for a single moment which totally unifies experience, for sexual ecstasy promises such a unitary moment. But as we shall see in our study of the cultural forms of hope, the linear vision reaching into the future is as unifying as is the total moment, though in a different way. This linear vision, springing from the biology of sex and yet reaching beyond it, is the one that needs to be clarified and emphasized today.

A FRAMEWORK FOR INTERPRETATION: WHITEHEAD'S PHILOSOPHY

Before we turn to the cultural dimension of hope, it is important to explore the setting of the biological thrust into the future by sexual reproduction in a wider understanding of the physical world. This is a most complex question, to which our answers must often be tentative. At the same time, the question is a real one that we must try to face.

The problem of the relation of such a human stance as hope to the workings of the physical world is almost impossible of solution if we are bound to the presuppositions of most modern science and theology. For both of these disciplines have for the most part accepted a total separation between the subjective and objective worlds, so that a "subjective" reality

such as purpose or hope could have nothing to do with what
can be observed objectively. Both the immense success of the
scientific method in explaining, without recourse to subjectivity or purpose, and the desire to free theology from conflict
with the details of scientific findings have pressed these two
disciplines so far apart that they have almost no ground for
common dialogue. The reasons for this split lie in the history
of philosophy, above all in the critical work of Hume and
Kant, who proved how different the objective and subjective
sides of reality are. Furthermore, Darwin's work and its
further developments have shown that a detailed purposeful
design determined in advance is not a meaningful way of interpreting the evolution of life.

In spite of all this history, the divorce between objectivity
and subjectivity is an impasse, for our commonsense perception of the world shows us that subjectivity and objectivity interact—our intentions result in action. And the pressing practical problems of our, or any, time cannot be met without bringing the two together, even if only pragmatically. Hope and
purpose must have something to do with an objective, external
world, if they are to be trusted.

It is possible to confront this impasse, and the most con-
structive approach is along the lines worked out by Alfred
North Whitehead.[11] Whitehead was able to accept the sharp
distinction, which Kant had stressed, between subjectivity and
objectivity without letting them fall apart. His central insight
was that neither subjectivity nor objectivity are enduring realities, but that they alternate as aspects of the concrete occasions which are real. Reality is not smoothly continuous in a
preformed time and space, as it had been supposed to be in
the Newtonian model. Rather, it consists of an infinitely
complex sequence of successive actual occasions. Each actual
occasion is both subjective and objective. Each occasion,
whether an occasion at the very simplest subatomic level or an
occasion in my conscious experience, has subjectivity in its
unique moment of concrescence or coming-to-be (though in

the simpler grades of occasions, of course, the subjective elements of freedom and purpose are trivial). Each occasion derives its data from the now objectively real (because completed) preceding occasions and in its turn becomes objectively real as a datum for later occasions. Although there are immense differences in the complexity of actual occasions, in principle subjectivity and objectivity thus are aspects of all reality. Purpose, associated with subjectivity, is directly known to us only in our own experience, but it is seen to be a characteristic, in varying degrees, of the subjectivity of all occasions. The efficient causality of previous occasions which shapes the feeling or "prehension" of new occasions, is likewise a characteristic of all reality. Freedom and purpose always operate within the limitations set for a given occasion by its data.

Such a perspective is congenial for exploring the problem we have set. Since it does not recognize a sharp line of distinction between living and nonliving or between human and nonhuman reality, at least the question whether a human reality such as hope can be related to the physical universe is a meaningful question in this perspective.

For the question of hope, it is important to see that Whitehead worked out his vision of reality as process not only to bring subjectivity and objectivity into some intelligible relationship, but also to take account of the forward movement of things in time. Mathematics and physics rather than biology were the scientific disciplines that brought his grasp of the problems into focus, but Whitehead was also deeply struck by the biological and evolutionary processes which have brought into being increasingly complex forms of existence with increasing amounts of freedom. The emergence of novelty was one of his central concerns, and he did not think that novelty could be accounted for apart from the aims of actual occasions at intensity of experience both in their own coming to be and in their relevant future, that is, their foreseeable possible impact on later occasions. Thus the aim of the present toward the future is a central feature of his vision, a feature that quite notably sets it apart from the many systems which have essentially static views of reality. But the aim at the future is, so to speak, decentralized and localized in the actual occasions themselves. There is no one fixed aim in detail for the whole of things, but there are specific aims of specific occasions. While these are taken up in turn (felt or "prehended") by succeeding occasions, each occasion has its own privacy and freedom, and does, within limits, set its own aim.

But the coherence and order that we experience are not adequately understood merely in terms of localized and decentralized seeking of aims by actual occasions, even if these do have to express some continuity because of the influence of past occasions on them. When novelty emerges it is related in an orderly way to previously existing order. Whitehead saw that this interrelationship between order and novelty required that there be an actual entity which offers to each occasion its initial aim, and which sets the initial aim in terms of the maximum intensity of contrasting unity which is possible for that occasion in that situation. The actual entity which does this, of course, is God. God's further function, to be discussed later, is to preserve the achievements of all actual occasions.

We shall examine the meaning of Whitehead's view of God for an understanding of hope in later chapters. Here we note only one point: God is the source of the aim toward the future, but Whitehead is resolutely pluralistic in his view of reality; each actual occasion has freedom, within limits, to set its own subjective aim, by modifying the initial aim given it by God. God does not determine the outcome; his power is the power of persuasion. How extensive and effective the power of divine persuasion can be is one of the central questions for a process theology of hope, and a question to which we must return.

For the moment another consequence of the process perspective must be emphasized: both God and the actual occasions are involved in process. This means that whereas our unreflective experience of subjectivity is of *continuing* subjectivity, in reality the continuing identity of a subject in time is a derivative rather than an ultimate reality. Just as experience comes in "droplets" or "buds," in discrete bits, the real subject (or self) is the subject of each bit of experience. The ultimately real subject is the concrescing occasion. Continuing identity in time is to be understood as a "personal order" of actual occasions, in which each successive occasion inherits from its predecessor. It is clear that this system could allow for greater or less importance for personal continuity in time, and that a use of Whitehead's thought to explore the meaning of Christian existence will find this question of continuing personal identity a central one.[12] But it is important as well to note that the paradigm of hope which we have used (the child) affirms that hope is not merely based on the continuation of personal identity. If one can look for some equivalent to the "child," then the death of one personally ordered sequence of occasions is not in itself a reason for abandoning hope.

Whitehead's vision affirms as fundamentally real some things that run counter to widespread scientific presuppositions; his work was a resolute effort to alter the scientific perspective. Basic to his view is the conviction that there is a tendency in things toward complexity and intensity, which runs counter to the tendency in measurable concentrations of energy to dissipate or "run down." The second law of thermodynamics (entropy tends toward a maximum) suggests that the physical universe is headed toward an eventual increase of disorder or randomness to the point where significant concentrations of energy will finally no longer eixst. Life is an important instance of a tendency in the other direction—toward the intensification of energy. Instead of seeing life as an accident or aberration, Whitehead saw it as a striking instance of a creativity that is everywhere at work. He speaks of a "three-fold urge: (i) to live, (ii) to live well, (iii) to live better. In fact the art of life is *first* to be alive, *secondly* to be alive in a satisfactory way, and *thirdly* to acquire an increase in satisfaction." [13] Final causation, or purpose—the central way in which we men experience what life is—is not to be understood either as an illusion (as in a mechanistic interpretation) or as a uniquely human property. Our experiences of purposeful action, on the contrary, supply us with the clue to an aspect of all actual occasions. Furthermore, "purpose" is not adequately conceived as the limited response of seeking a definite goal (purposing to cook a meal or do a day's work). Such a view of purpose is too static. Purpose tends beyond the known model that it is striving to achieve. The tendency of purposive action continually to reach beyond its original models or goals is the great evidence of human creativity, and Whitehead took it as an instance of a far more widespread creativity.

The evolution of life is one of the most striking instances of a pattern of continually reaching beyond an existing and functioning model, and experimenting with new forms. A central question of biology has been whether this evolutionary questing can be understood in terms of purpose. Since sexual reproduction is a central feature of the process of most evolutionary development, the tantalizing question is raised whether there is any connection between the phenomenon of hope in concern for the child and the evolutionary questing for a "better" form of life.   1652028

Most of the current interpretation of evolution would reject such questions out of hand. The attempt to view evolution in terms of an *élan vital* has not stood up. Most students of evolution see no need to bring in any element of purpose. Natural selection working on chance variation within the gene pool of a population seems a sober and adequate approach to most. The brilliant research on the structure and function of the DNA molecule has not been carried out with models that include any element of purpose. Furthermore, more generally it can be said that many activities of living organisms which seem purposive to us are better explained simply as repetitions of successful innovations. In spite of the fact that purpose or final causation is uncongenial to most current interpretation of evolution, however, from the point of view of the perspective we have outlined it can be seen to play a real and central role, along with chance and efficient causation.[14]

"Life is a passage from physical order to pure mental originality, and from pure mental originality to canalized mental originality. It must also be noted that the pure mental originality works by the canalization of relevance from the primordial nature of God. Thus an originality in the temporal world is conditioned, though not determined, by an initial subjective aim supplied by the ground of all order and of all originality." [15] The technical Whiteheadian vocabulary is making the point that an element of purpose ("pure mental originality") is involved in the emergence of novelty, and that if it is to persist, the novelty must be stabilized ("canalized"); if this occurs, it may become the basis for further originality. The foci of living energy at various levels of complexity have an aim at intensity; their departures from established patterns are not *merely* random but involve *also* the intention of increasing the kind of satisfaction that is appropriate for them.[16] This does not mean that the various constituent parts intend the development of the emerging creature, but that in the complex processes of development which result in a variety of living creatures, the tendency toward intensity of experience is at work, and specifically at work in the actual foci of experience at various levels in each organism. "Viewed this way, evolution appears as *a general movement toward societies of organisms with more complex mentality*, even though the movement has been sporadic and never has had any one type of organism as its goal." [17] In this general sense there is a connection between the thrust toward the future which we see in the child and which becomes conscious in human culture on the one hand, and the process of biological evolution on the other.

It is important not to try to make this argument prove too much. Since this concept of purpose is coherent with the freedom of the actual occasions, no one outcome (e.g., man)

could have been the predefined purpose of the whole process
—though once man has come to be the particular form of life
peculiarly susceptible to intensity of experience, to freedom,
and to the reach toward the future, it is not unreasonable to
see him as of special meaning because of his potentialities.
Beyond this, there is no reason to suppose that any one form
of order will last perpetually; the question remains to be discussed whether and in what ways the forms that pass away
can be understood as still contributing to the future. We have
already noted, in considering the symbol "child," the immense
amount of "waste" in the process of life, and this same impres-
sion is left by a survey of the evolutionary process. The individual is not important from the point of view of the devel-
oping species; many lines of evolutionary development "fail,"
and most seem to show a tendency to become static after a
time of development. Thus any attempt to correlate man's
drive toward the future with that which is discernible in the
development of life must deal seriously with waste and loss.

Once this sober fact is accepted, however, it does seem rea-
sonable to affirm that the alternation between intensity of the
moment and concern for the future, so characteristic of human
experience, is also characteristic of a much wider sphere. We
see this alternation most clearly, beyond ourselves, in other
living things. But we shall be on soundest ground if we follow
Whitehead, and interpret also the inorganic realm as dimly
characterized by subjectivity as well. The alternation between
two phases of experience is basic; both are essential. But what
appears from this survey of the physical rootage of our nature
is that while the thirst for totality, for the infinite, is a basic
and wonderful part of our makeup, it tends to claim more for
itself than it really can achieve. Total unity is of the moment,
and the other element of longing, the longing for the "more" of
the future, is if anything more essential.

II

The Creative Act

THE TENSION BETWEEN THE DEFINITE AND THE INFINITE

Like sex, any human act of cultural creativeness embodies both a quest for infinity and a quest for definite form. The two quests, taken together, express a forward movement of life into the future, and the relation of hope to the creative act is a vital one, despite the fact that so much of the creative work of our own time seems to reflect more despair than hope.

If the creative act, in its reaching for infinity, loses its focus on the definite and finite created form, it also loses its contact with hope. The longing for "all," and even the longing for "more, more," can overwhelm the motor of hope that is part of the creative act. The longing for infinity may be a necessary phase of the imagination of our time, but it is a serious mistake to see it as a real opening to the future.

The previous chapter has shown that hope arises, at the preconscious level, as a response to the forward-moving and open-ended processes of biological growth and (especially) sexual reproduction. The new generation's hope for its own growth, and even more the channeling of energy by parents to support the existence and growth of the new generation, are the biological origins of hope. This way of beginning has the merit of recognizing that much of the substance of hope is widely present—almost universally present—in human life, even though conscious hope that can be expressed is much more limited in scope.

Now we turn to human cultural creativity, and we shall find that it too implies and is supported by a forward movement of life into the future, even though many forms of creative action do not bring this forward movement to consciousness. Creativeness is far more persistent than hope, but it requires an openness to the future that is the basis for hope. Not *because* he hopes does man create, but by creating he comes to be involved in the open future, which at a certain level of awareness can come to consciousness as hope.

THE MAKING OF THINGS

Consider a simple type of creativeness: the making of things. An Indian woman is making pots. Each pot is a new thing. Creativeness means the appearance of new concrete organizations of the existing materials. Probably in archaic societies the consciousness of the artisan is fixed almost entirely on the repetitive aspect of creativity—on making a pot just like other pots. The amazing persistence of the techniques by which things are made testifies to the highly repetitive style of creative work in pretechnological societies. And the focus of creative consciousness on repetition is supported by the widespread archaic view that creative acts are repetitions of the primordial creation: men do what the gods did in the beginning. But even viewed in this framework, each new pot is a new creation, a new concrete existence and an object of joy as such.

Furthermore, the styles of pottery change, and often change, even in very stable societies, with surprising rapidity. Here there is at work an impetus to make a *different* thing. Even in the most traditional societies, and probably often unconsciously, there is an appeal of finding a new way of "saying" what a pot "says." Though the conscious model of the creative act may be that of repeating the original creation, the actual performance has room for the emergence of new styles. The claim of the new in the sense of the "different," the style that has not been expressed, is an inexorable claim of human creativeness, and its functioning, albeit slowly, even where thinking about the creative making of things has no place for novelty, is all the more powerful testimony to its importance in understanding the creative act.

True enough, the new style may be new only in a very short-run view. Not only in so compact an instance as the style of pottery, but also in much more complex expressions of cultural style, there are frequent cases of oscillation between two extremes, where the short-range impulse may be the lure of what is different, but the long-range result seems to be a relentless swing of the pendulum between two opposing possibilities—classical and romantic, say, or ideational and sensate. But such an oscillating view of cultural change can ultimately be held only by means of abstraction. The concrete things made are not the same as those of an earlier version of the repeated style. It can be added that any creative action that tries to make a sharp break with its past in order to express the "different" will quickly fall into the likelihood of repeating some earlier forms, or else of losing much of the complexity and intensity expressed in its past. Quite to the contrary of much contemporary sensibility, an awareness of the past is a powerful aid toward novelty rather than an obstacle to it.

The next question is whether, beyond the thrust toward a "different" thing, there is a thrust toward a "better" thing. From our example of pots we might note that pots with spouts have been made for over five thousand years, yet most of the spouts still drip. It is a serious question whether the different is better. The question can be broken down into two: whether the thing is better in itself and whether it is better for something.

The second question looks at the thing in terms of its value for some purpose beyond itself. There is no doubt that men try to make things that are in this sense "better," that are more functional for some use, despite the example of dripping spouts cited above and despite the complex of other factors that go into determining how things are made in a given society. The real problem for the future dimension of the creative act at this point arises from the interaction of different functions in social or individual life. Advances in medicine and public health enable men to live better, but against this improved functioning is the other functioning that leads to the population explosion. The automobile is made better for transportation, but it thereby becomes far more effective in polluting the atmosphere. The acts of creative man, questing for the "better," make clear the interactive and mutually responsible nature of creative action, and remind us (if we need the reminder) that the quest for the better is not a way out of the precariousness of existence. The fear that the mutual interrelatedness of value scales poses an impossible problem has much to do with the randomness and rebellion against form in much contemporary creative action.

But this threat that the quest for the better may be self-destructive can honestly be regarded as an open problem rather than an insoluble one. The question will reappear here in the chapter on secularization. If the problem can be seen as open, then the basic thrust of creativeness—to make things that are better for some function—does not have to be shifted from the idiom of hope to that of despair.

The other way of asking whether a pot or any created thing is "better" asks whether there is some way of judging the products of man's creative action simply in terms of their own excellence or beauty. Many would say that although such a question can be asked, it cannot be answered. For, they say, the excellence or beauty of an object is so fully a matter of subjective preference that some simply like one thing and some another. This view correctly points to the fact that there are infinite possibilities of excellence or beauty. But excellence or beauty cannot simply be dismissed as matters of emotional preference. For to do so overlooks two factors that are basic in the quest for excellence: the quest for form and the quest for expression of reality. Each brings the quest for excellence out of the purely emotive realm.

The quest for form, many-sided as it is, involves a joy in complexity and in harmoniously related complexity of form. In a study of this theme, Gregor Sebba contrasts the structure of the folk poem "Yankee Doodle" with Goethe's lyric, "Über allen Gipfeln"; the interwoven complexity of sound and meaning in the latter make it, as a creation of form, of far greater excellence than the folk poem.[1]

For a study of hope and the future, the perplexing thing about the lure of excellence of form in creation is that any given type or genre of creative action has limited possibilities. After a time most of them have been exhausted, and the form cannot be elaborated without mere repetition. Indeed, one clue to the impact of form is precisely through its "deformation" of the expected structure, through its being different or new. When a type of form has been thoroughly worked out it affords little opportunity for the impact of surprise by "deformation." The rebellion against form in creative work may be thought of as an attempt to escape from form into sheer energy, but if it is to be fruitful, the rebellion against exhausted form has to lead to the discovery of new forms or to a higher synthesis of already known forms. This aspect of the quest for form—the need for disclosure by deformation—provides a problem that needs to be thought through for any perspective on the creative act which, as in Christianity, is linked with forms definitively shaped in the past. This problem will appear again in our discussion of the figure of Christ.

Form as disclosure leads beyond the quest for form to the quest for expression of reality. Here there is a convergence of the two meanings of "better," intrinsic excellence and instrumental functioning. For as expression, the created thing is intrinsically related to the experience or reality that it expresses. Works of human creativeness do not simply copy what they express, useful as the Platonic theory of art as representation or copying is for an understanding of some phases of art. What the created work does is to establish a little world of its own, which is in some way a comment on the world as otherwise known, the "real world." A drama simplifies and heightens the action by which it makes its point. All such works, in addition, are relative to their particular historical situations and to particular visions of the world. The various strivings for the better do not necessarily point to one "best." But the diversity of creative expression can be grouped into styles, and some styles and some expressions are more adequate in confronting us with the claim of a particular style of existence. The infinitely varied expressions of the creative quest can thus be ordered, and the quest for the better is seen to be not merely private and emotive, but a search that corresponds to alternative ways of perceiving the structure of the world. These in turn are not simply arbitrary, but, so far as the conditions of human existence are concerned, can be sorted out into a limited number of types. Bold as it is to affirm this, it nevertheless appears that the types of structures through which existence is perceived can in turn be ranked in a scale of ascending complexity, though not (so far as our present situation is concerned) into a single series leading to a single most excellent type.

Can anything more be said about whether the quest for the "better" points toward a "best"? It seems that there are three alternatives: either there is no goal for the quest for the better, or the quest is ultimately a temporary thing, so that the final "best" is the undifferentiated being out of which the various concrete existences arise and into which they sink again, or the vision of a convergent best represents something real. With a qualification, we opt for the third position. In passing, it is important to note that the hope for the final and ultimate "best" has had immense pragmatic results by leading men to seek a higher synthesis of the various forms of the "better" which in the present seem to be irreconcilable. But this third possibility in turn needs to be broken down into two: the view that there will (or at least may) be a single convergent unifying point (as in traditional Christian eschatology and in Teilhard de Chardin), and the more pluralistic view that in the continuing quest for the unifying best there are both convergences and also ultimately irreconcilable varieties of the "better." We hold that the potent symbol of the unifying point, the ultimate "best," does express something real, but that it has to be recognized as a symbol that promises more than it can deliver. There can be many unifications of the lines of seeking the better, but there will also always be the need to sacrifice one good thing in order that another may be.

We may sum it up by saying that while there is genuine creativity in simply making a "new" thing, the distinctive nuances of the human creative act come out in the effort to make a "different" thing and a "better" thing. The terms "different" and "better," in their comparative form, bring out the point, so often neglected today, that creativeness is a cultural process; its openness to the future is not found through isolation from the past, but by reaction to and interaction with the rich store of possibilities already worked out. The creative act, and the culture that emerges from it, provide a substratum of motion toward complexity and intensity which can come to consciousness as hope. Hope can appear only if men believe that the possibilities for new creativeness have not been exhausted, and that the different lines of creative action do not have to destroy each other.

THE CREATIVE ACT AND THE DEFINITE

"New," "different," and "better" are finite terms; "best" can also be a finite term, the end of a finite series. But "best" can easily be thought of as escaping beyond the finite and being qualitatively different. As was suggested above, "best" is the term which, from a perspective of hope, has to be treated with the greatest reserve. For the escape into the infinite is the great temptation (or should one more dispassionately say, the great alternative) to the modern man who is trying to see whether there can be any basis for hope. We may clarify the alternatives by seeing how time is perceived in relation to creativeness. In his *Christ and Apollo*, William F. Lynch contrasts "the steady march of the soul through irrevocable events" to the flight from time which is so characteristic of many recent creative visions. Time has to be entered into as the acceptance of the definite if a landscape is to appear which has a horizon of hope.[2] For it is only by receiving *this* definite if fleeting moment as the focus of a unique creative act that the future can be open to the new concrete possibilities which may appear in it. Resistance to the concrete confrontation with time may take different forms. In contrast to the escape into an interior timeless imagination, which is typical of many European efforts to destroy time, the American style has been a frenzied activity which uses up time. But neither effort to escape the narrow, concrete, finite series of events which make up an actual life can be a gateway to hope. Only in and through the definite can there be a real openness to the future. Escape from time may lead to tranquillity, but not to hope.

No doubt we stand at a time when both the forms of social structure and the forms of imagination require a drastic reshaping. So far as the perception of time is concerned, the alienation arising from loss of any chance to be creative in their work by so many in a technological society is close to the source of much of the protest. There is a close link between the repetitive and traditional crafts and the creation of the fresh and different, as shown above. But when the making of things is mechanized and dissected into tiny, endlessly repeated operations in which the human contribution is mechanical, then functional participation in production cannot express creativeness, and work does not disclose any meaningful and definite moments of time or any progression through time. To meet the alienation arising from loss of creative function in work is a fundamental demand on plans for social change, more fundamental in the long run than the maintenance of a particular standard of living. There are hopeful possibilities here as well as extremely discouraging ones.

The most obvious rejection of time in our culture is the rejection of the past. It is striking that in so much creative thought and expression in the arts, in the revolutionary politics of the young and the dispossessed, and in the vision of a more humane world, most of the important voices speak in terms of an abrupt break with the past or a reversal of the past. Here we must distinguish sharply between a practical program for the present moment and an effort to understand the process of creative change. There are often convincing reasons in practical and pragmatic terms for speaking of an abrupt or total break with the past, but it does not follow that such rhetoric takes account of all that is actually going on in the situation.

We can better understand the rejection of the past as part of a vital contribution to creativeness by returning to Ernst Bloch's insight that the daydreams of children are one of the best avenues to understanding what it is to be open to the future. Such dreams are full of creative imagination. Different as they are in different societies and in different parts of one society, these hopeful dreams are full—as dreams, not as reality, of course—of the active side of creativity as well as of receptiveness to what is expected to come or to be given. They are full of ego, of "what I will do." This point was noted in the previous chapter. A different aspect is important here. Whatever the lack to which it responds, such a vision looks for a complete resolution. "They lived happily ever after," the stylized ending for a children's story, reflects the character of a child's spontaneous imagination. Children can easily think of a total solution to their problems, a total fulfillment of their dreams, while the adult's dream of a better world comes to be more limited.

The longing for a perfect and total fulfillment is connected with an imperfectly formed sense of time in children. "Why can't it stay?" In a sense the problem of growing up is the

problem of learning to cope with the fact that things never do
stay. Yet the intuition of the adult also cries out deeply for
something that will not erode with time, and the daydreams of
children, still innocent of the pressure of time, bring this longing to expression more fully than adult imagination can do. To
put it differently, the child's imagination can reach without
strain to his infinity. As we become older, we realize how far
beyond us is any particular vision of infinity that we try to approach.

There are various ways of responding to the increasing
distance between the total resolution of the daydream and the
inexorable flow of time that breaks life into small bits and
seems to pull the present away from the past and make the future so problematic. But the call for a total break with the past
can easily be an expression of a refusal to face the definiteness
of time, a utopian assertion of a total solution that will not face
the limitations imposed on reality by what has already happened. The creative transition out of the daydream means focusing it on the definite, hard as this is to do. Particularly in a
transitional time such as ours, when inherited forms of the
imagination are breaking up, creativeness often tries to escape
from the definite toward the vague indefinite. This reminds us
that the imagination requires some framework of meaning if it
is to reach forward creatively into the future. It is not accidental that Father Lynch, whose probing study of the contrast between the focus on the definite (symbolized by Christ) and
the vague ideal (symbolized by Apollo) which we have mentioned, joins his treatment of the fruitfulness of a definite
focus of the imagination with a discussion of the theological
theme of analogy. The sheer unrelated definite is significant,
probably, only as it becomes a symbol, by repetition, of the indefinite or infinite. The freedom and fullness of imagination
that come from concentrating on the definite can function only
when the definite is recognized as "belonging." We are in a
transitional period, but that makes it all the more important to
see this point, which can be put in traditional terms by saying

that if there is no doctrine of God it is most difficult to find a
meaningful doctrine of man and the world.

It is hardly necessary to document the dissatisfaction with
the definite in much contemporary work of the imagination. If
definite traditional forms appear, they may be treated with
scorn or parody. The art of our time tends (in old-fashioned
Kantian terms) away from "beauty" (which has form) toward
the "sublime" (which is infinite and chaotic), though where
Kant saw the sublime predominantly in nature, our time finds
the chaotic and infinite in man. In the previous chapter the
tension between form and the chaotic appeared, and there it
was noted that the quest for an unmediated confrontation
with the infinite was the driving force of much of our culture's
preoccupation with sex, and also that sex, if dissociated from
the definite and creaturely symbol of the child, easily becomes
an attempt at a gnostic flight into the undifferentiated all, parallel to the flight into death. The longing to escape from a concrete ego, and to experience a loss of the line of separation between self and other, is clearly interpreted by Norman O.
Brown as a regression to the undifferentiated point of
beginning.[3] We may sympathize with his revolt against the
definiteness of moralistic rigidity, but the solution to the isolation and ingrown self-preoccupation of the ego does not have
to be loss of center. There is also the possibility of a turning
outward, and a functional focus toward the future. We have
shown above that the child is the truly future-oriented sexual
symbol, and only the concrete and definite presence of the
child, or of some symbolic equivalent, can transform the longing to escape fron ingrown self-preoccupation away from the
regressive return to the point of origin and forward toward the
future.

The same is the case with the future-oriented daydream, the
utopian vision of which finds freest expression in the fancy of
childhood. This too is quickly transformed into a return to the
point of beginning, since only there is a total resolution imag-
inable. But the other and better alternative is to turn its ener-

gies forward into a concrete and definite product, a creative work. Creativeness means bringing a vision to expression. One function of the vision is to present a reality concrete enough to be expressed; another is to point to the inexpressible beyond. If either function is lost, creativeness suffers; in particular, if the concrete moment and work lose significance, the "beyond" to which the creative vision points loses all connection with the future and can only be a glimpse of the primordial and undifferentiated whole.

It is foolish for the college professor to think that he should tell people with creative imagination how they should use it. But the professor may nevertheless make an honest comment on what is going on. The comment is not intended to be a call for a return to a previous concept of order within which men found creative freedom. The breakup of known forms is a call for new ones. "One decisive mark of the modern world is its will," as Thomas J. J. Altizer remarks, "to break or transcend all previous limits placed upon the condition of man or society." [4] The breakdown of traditional forms is part of the contemporary quest for an expansion of consciousness that will bring consciousness into the undifferentiated realm, into the indefinite infinite that cannot be contained in any form. The new movements toward randomness of form, as in the randomly composed music of John Cage, can bring an experience akin to *satori*, the enlightenment of Zen. Narrative writing in its own way, by its rejection of plot and character, strongly shows the breakup of the world and the self alike. All these expressions can be taken, in their lack of consecutiveness, of humanly visible order or sequence, as ways of presenting something like the child's innocence of time.

Such an effort may succeed in bringing to expression a quite new vision of the world. But if the new world vision remains fixed on lack of order and randomness, its goal will be tranquillity rather than hope, as noted above. To make hope viable, some new forms of order will have to emerge, since only within them will the self be able to concentrate on the definite and finite as the stage or step in time which is liberating now because it is felt to have its place.

But we suspect that the move toward an Eastern tranquillity, and an Eastern undifferentiated absolute, is premature as an expression of creativeness. Much as this style of life has to teach us, we are not at a point where all our vitality can be transferred into this framework. In one area, the typical Western drive toward continuing expansion as a way of grasping the movement to the future has already received a decisive check: the check to our economic-technological expansion from the threat of ecological imbalance and destruction. This blow at a widely received if not profound form of future orientation could easily be taken as an indication that we should turn to a timeless, nondeveloping, and hopefully tranquil style of life. But there is no workable return to pretechnological and nonchanging forms of social life, despite the experiments of some communal groups. The unmet claims of the world's community call for a future-oriented approach. Instead of groping for a static and tranquil life-style as a reaction to the ecological crisis, it is wiser to see this crisis as something which brings the American dream of expansion out of the infinite into the finite by ruthless necessity. The unquestioned assumptions of technological and economic development have been in harmony with the spirit of our culture, and have been part of the movement to "break and transcend all the limits placed upon the condition of man and society." We now know that this vision of endless expansion was a delusion, even though we have just begun to rethink economic theory on the basis of the new insights. The implications of ecology for the wider reaches of creativity have been even less well worked out, but they point also to a renewed focus on the definite and finite as the focus of creativeness. No doubt there is a powerful longing for the past to which we cannot return in much of the current writing on ecology. But an ecologically sensitive creativeness must not turn away from the future. The shift in perspective required is a recognition that creative action is not necessarily a movement of expansion, but can take place within a sober recognition of the limits set for the new, and through a questing for the particular and limited goal that will effectively bring the new into being.

Thus the movement toward a new definite ordering of things is the movement of human creativeness, a movement that need not rebel at vast amounts of repetitiveness in being creative, but one that also has room for infinite variety. This is the general dimension of human creativeness, a dimension that has many analogies to the biological creativity discussed in the first chapter. Such creativeness need not be understood in an elitist fashion. Our original illustration of pottery-making was chosen to show that creativeness is by no means the monopoly of the gifted few. And the same is true in the realm of interpersonal relations, a realm that is the place for much if not most human creativeness, in which each meeting of "I" and "thou" contains all the newness of a new creation.

CREATIVENESS AND RECEPTIVITY

Some people object to making creativeness central to understanding man's hope, because the opportunities for creativeness are so largely excluded for many, particularly as a result of the mechanization of work in a technological society. To this we returned the answer that it is possible to have a sober hope that man will learn to use technology in more human ways. Perhaps this hope is strengthened if we recognize the point just made, that creativeness is not the property of a few geniuses, but is a universal possibility, while at the same time many of its expressions will be transient and repetitive. Creativeness is a basic human capacity with a wide range of possible expression.

We now turn to an opposite objection to making creativeness central in interpreting human hope. To think from human existence toward hope along the theme of creativeness seems highly questionable to many because such an approach seems to allow too little place for the stance of receptiveness or in religious terms, faith. To approach hope through creativeness may sound like making the future man's achievement. For the early modern period, the creativeness of reason was especially subject to theological suspicion—the whore Reason, as Luther called it. Since that time the "Faustian" exaggeration of the ego as the center of creativeness has made many who stand both in and out of the theological tradition eager to find a more fundamental level of humanness than the ego-active consciousness that is often understood to be the creative center of man.

We have already touched on this problem in Chapter I, where we examined the "deficiency-cognition" of Abraham Maslow and affirmed that an orientation based on it is a one-sided basis for hope. In other terms, we do not find it possible to understand creativeness within the scope of goal-directed, deficiency-oriented striving. Equally important in creativeness is the experience of being "given" the new creation. Receptivity is as central in creativeness as is activity.

So far as the theological side of this discussion is concerned, the root of the misguided separation of God's creativeness and man's creativeness has been a wrong notion of God's transcendence, as we shall try to show in the next chapter. The feeling that God must somehow represent a totality has made it impossible to allow his creativeness to interwork with human creativeness. Against this widely held view it must be stated that, in the traditional vocabulary, justification by faith does not express the whole of the relation between God and man. It is precisely the interworking of man's activity and receptivity in his creativeness that needs to be illuminated by the interworking of God's and man's creativeness. The sense that the new creation or newly established relationship is "given" more than "produced" is widely testified to in all fields of creativeness. But it has been an impoverishment of faith rather than the opposite to translate this insight about creativeness into a theological idiom which completely separates the work of God and man. God's proper place is not infringed by recognizing that he can and does share his creativeness with man. The fact that faith itself can only be expressed by means of some expression of man's creativeness should make clear the profoundly interlocked character of the relation between the two contributions to creation.

So far as the widespread reaction against the modern exaggeration of the ego is concerned, here just as in theology we need to avoid a one-sided extreme. The self cannot escape from its prison of ego by moving to a pure state of egoless receptivity, except as a momentary solution. Pure receptivity, like pure activity, is an abstraction. Actual creative activity involves an oscillation or combining alternation of both poles.

CREATIVENESS AND PROCESS THOUGHT

Human creativeness can be understood fruitfully in many frameworks. But it should be clear that process thought illuminates those aspects of creativeness which have been stressed here. In Whiteheadian thought, creativity is one of the ultimates, one of the fundamental characteristics of reality. We have used the more concrete term "creativeness" to express the form or manifestation of creativity that is important in human culture. The sketch of Whitehead's view of God and process given at the end of the former chapter provided a framework in which the various aspects of human creativeness emphasized above will appear as particular expressions of a wider reality.

There is one important way in which human creativeness is an indirect product of the basic creativity expressed in all reality. The fundamental creation is self-creation, guided by the persuasion of God. Each occasion is *causa sui*, "its own cause," as Whitehead puts it. But the kinds of human cultural creativity that we have discussed bring into being not simply a new occasion, but a symbolic expression of something highly valued by the creator. They are ways of preserving something

seen so that it can be recovered or seen again by a later
occasion in the life of the same person or by another. But
granting this indirectness of human works to the living processes from which they arise, the character of the process is
most illuminating in understanding why creativeness functions
as it does.

Creativeness is expressed in a definite object or relationship.
It is the definite occasion that is real, and the stress we have
laid upon the definite in creativeness is justified by the fact
that the finite occasion is the real. Yet the act of bringing the
new into being arises from the lure both of the new definite
creation that is coming into being and of the infinite field of
possibilities beyond it. That each occasion is free, and that its
aim is derived from a related group of relevant possibilities
provided for it by God, is the background of this interplay between the definite and the infinite in creativeness. That creativeness finds much of its satisfaction in repetitive acts
(making pots, in our illustration, or cooking meals, or teaching
classes), yet also involves the lure of the different or better:
these facts find meaning from the same background. The willingness to joy in the definite rather than to long for the "all" is
a recognition of the central reality of the actual occasion. That
creativeness tends to be impoverished if it loses contact with
the possibilities worked out in the past is also illuminated
from a process point of view, which affirms that each occasion
is shaped by its relevant past.

Creativeness turns the creator outward; it is not simply an
expression of concern for ego. In fact, the act of creation
brings an awareness that the created form and newness sought
for are both one's own most intimate contribution and also a
gift that "comes." This widely sensed perception of creativeness as both *done* and *given* is illuminated by the process view
that God leads occasions to enact themselves and gives them
an aim at their highest possibilities, but that the occasions
have their moment of freedom to become what they choose to
be.

While the terrible and destructive possibilities of competitiveness between different lines of creative activity are patent, they can be accepted in hope if one sees that creativeness fundamentally involves a drive to reach a higher synthesis of competing possibilities, even though this synthesis is not always possible.

CREATIVENESS AND HOPE

The creative act or encounter, immensely varied as it is, receives its impulse from the incomplete or potential, the "not yet." Hope is a much more specific relation to the "not yet." If the self is passive in relation to the coming future, hope erodes. If the potential future has no order and is simply vague and indefinite, hope is likewise excluded, though tranquillity may be the fruit of an effort at understanding and faith. But creativeness, if it can be understood in a setting that allows both for the genuine spontaneity of the creative act and for a meaningful framework of limitation open toward the future, does function as an indispensable basis for hope. For hope cannot exist indefinitely as a simply passive virtue. It belongs in a world where man's creativeness and God's creativeness are known to respect and to be significant for each other. The view of creativeness that we have sketched above sees it as an essentially open process. God cannot determine the outcome of human creativeness, nor set for himself an immutable goal. Creativeness may go astray, turn stale or demonic, or be frustrated in finding expression. But hope does not require an assurance of a particular outcome. It is far more central to hope to believe that the definite moments and definite created realities are taken seriously both by men and by God, than to believe that a particular promise is assured in advance. But this raises a question that we shall have to probe more deeply later: the relation between precariousness and loss on the one hand, and some assurance that the moment is taken up into a continuing reality on the other.

III

The Infinite

EROSION OF THE TRADITIONAL WESTERN VIEW
OF THE INFINITE

Both in the discussion of sex and in the discussion of creativeness it has been shown that the "infinite" is a problematic notion, and one that threatens the forward movement of life which takes place through definite and limited moments into the future. Since hope can flourish only in the latter setting, it is important now to examine the place of the infinite in the theology and in the imagination of our culture.

"There is but one only living and true God, who is infinite in being and perfection, . . . immutable, immense, eternal, incomprehensible, almighty, most wise, most holy, . . . most absolute. . . . God . . . is alone in and unto himself all-sufficient, not standing in need of any creatures which he hath made." (The Westminster Confession of Faith.) The majestic prose of the seventeenth century articulates the form of the infinite that has been the central one in shaping our imagination. Here the infinite is partly defined negatively (immutable, incomprehensible), but it is given positive character as an infinite extension of a group of experienced qualities that are of highest value (almighty, most wise, most holy). The reach away from man toward infinity is mysterious through the negative aspect of infinity, its opposition to whatever is limited, and its incomprehensibility. But the movement toward infinity is ordered by the fact that the beginning point of the reach is at least partly known. Wisdom, holiness, etc., are affirmed as really experienced in human life. The infinite is not just a negative or mysterious reality, despite the presence also of negative qualifications. Rather, the pressure or weight of the infinite is felt precisely by the fact that it is an infinite expansion of something fragmentarily known in our own experience. Against my wisdom, God's wisdom! Against my goodness, God's goodness! The immense power of this way of relating to the infinite can be seen especially in Protestantism. Guilt and creativeness alike are stimulated by the pressure of the infinite. Men feel guilty because they fall so far short of the infinite, and at the same time they may be pricked forward by the claim of the unfulfilled reach of the infinite qualities they already partly know. The tension between guilt and creativeness, so clear in the history, for instance, of American culture, arises from the incongruity between the finite creature and the infinite which can scarcely be felt other than as infinite demand. It is no accident—a point to which we shall return in our final chapter—that in this piety the saving element, the figure of Christ, is precisely a limitation upon God's infinity, a finite figure. The infinite in itself is all but unbearable.

The Calvinist doctrine of the sovereignty of God is the clearest expression of this way of being grasped by infinity. If God is infinite in power and glory, nothing can stand in his way. The consequences were worked out with stunning consistency. Despite the overrationalistic form of the supralapsarian-infralapsarian debates and of the controversies over the freedom of the will, this whole style of faith was at bottom driven by an intense sense of wonder and mystery, a sense of the illimitable mystery of God. In studies of American culture, it is the merit of Perry Miller's work on the Puritans and on Jonathan Edwards that he perceived this vital sense of mystery, a mystery surprisingly conferring dignity on human life, behind the formidable and now unfamiliar intellectual expressions through which it came to words. But the combination of fire and penetration in a thinker such as Jonathan Edwards brings to light precisely the problem of God's infinity con-

ceived as the infinite extension of what we experience as good
—the problem of competition between God and man. If God
is all-powerful, what is left for man? Edwards' honest answer
was: No freedom of the will, for God's power runs completely
through the sequence of causal determination, which exhaustively shapes man's actions. This was the only way he could
preserve without loophole the infiniteness of the God he
adored.

Edwards, like other Calvinists, was persuaded that such a
view left sufficient dignity for man, and it is better recognized
today that in its vital period the Calvinist tradition was an immensely productive stimulus to creativeness. But the one-
sided and unrelenting stress on the infinite power and glory of
God has led to a progressive rejection of this whole mode of
imagining the infinite, whether through the course of perceiving the demonic quality of such a sovereign infinity (Melville), or through the course of brushing aside the whole
seriousness of the question of ultimate mystery (Franklin).

Parenthetically, I should add that it is surprising that this
rigorous and sober view of wonder has not become the center
of a theological revival today. When there is so prevailing a
determinism in many scientific fields, there could well be a renewed, modern vision of the sovereignty of God in a universe
where human consciousness is strictly an epiphenomenon, a
by-product of the things that really act. Is the lack of such a
theology a sign of a failure of courage? Personally, I should be
very much inclined to explore this alternative if I were not
committed to the contrasting process view with its basic assumption of freedom and, within limits, indeterminacy.

A deterministic view of God's sovereignty has often been an
intense stimulus to creativeness. But we are now in a period of
strong reaction against the style of faith which is grounded on
the infinite majesty of God, a reaction incidentally testified to
by the fact that hardly any of the sympathetic and penetrating
studies of the Puritan culture which so valiantly wrestled with
the infinite God come from authors who have any commitment
to this kind of faith. The reaction against the infinite so con-

ceived arose from a sense of its repressiveness, its threat to freedom. A straight line runs from prophets of the repressiveness of God such as Blake and Melville to the "death of God" theology of today and to the less extreme perspective expressed by the slogans, "man on his own," and "man come of age." Apart from this line of theological development, it must not be forgotten that an immensely important consequence of God's infinity conceived as an infinite extension of qualities highly valued by man has been the stimulation of man to compete with God. Milton's Satan and Melville's Ahab remind us of the force of rebellious competition which the infinite God provoked. The overwhelming conclusion has been that despite their common term, a valued quality, the infinite and the finite so conceived are simply incompatible. If God competes with what men do, he can do it so much better that they lose significance; or, put the other way around, they can be their own finite selves with dignity only by getting rid of the infinite— and the infinite on the horizon may tempt them to exceed their finitude and reach for infinity themselves. This conclusion is consistent with what was shown in the earlier discussion of creativeness, that a focus on the infinite may lead to a loss of focus on the definite in the creative act.

The Infinite as the Indefinite

But the rejection of the infinite as the infinite extension of known values has not expelled the infinite from modern consciousness. There have been many who have tried to establish a purely finite and relative view of things, but the lure of the infinite has forcefully reasserted itself. In many different ways men have been trying to revisualize the infinite in a form older than the rejected form: to return to the ancient perception of the infinite as the indefinite. This was the way in which the infinite was first introduced into our thought by the Greeks. For Aristotle, for instance, the infinite was potential rather than actual, and undeterminate, and as such it could not be known, for knowledge requires form. Since Aristotle associated God with form and with perfection, and since the infinite by escaping form was neither perfect nor actual, for him infinity was not an attribute of God. It was the contact between the Greek effort to clarify the meaning of infinity and the Christian tradition in which the transcendent God was known as having definite qualities related to those of men that brought about the shift from the infinite as infinite potential to the form of infinity against which we are still reacting. Though the modern search has little direct contact, for the most part, with the earlier formulation of the infinite as the indefinite, much of the modern imagination has been rediscovering a vision of the indefinite infinite as the mystery beyond the concrete and formed reality which we experience. Thus a resurgence of an essentially archaic form of the infinite is under way. For beyond the abstract thought of the Greeks lies the archaic intuition of a primordial unformed totality out of which the actually existing world emerges.

The clearest form of the rediscovery of the indefinite infinite comes in the search to appropriate Eastern forms of understanding. Emerson, who inherited Edwards' sense of wonder, moved away from Edwards' version of the infinite toward an indefinite infinite which he was able to grasp partly because of the newly available Hindu thought. Since Emerson's time the influence of the East has become progressively stronger, and a battery of recent thinkers such as Alan Watts, Arnold Toynbee, F. C. S. Northrop, and Aldous Huxley have explored the ways of relating Western culture to an infinite which is undifferentiated and all-inclusive, and which relativizes the concrete manifestations of reality or regards them as illusion. Others have found something similar in the mystical tradition of the West; thus Richard Rubenstein, to whom we referred at the very beginning of the book, draws on the negative mysticism of Isaac Luria, a Spanish Jew of the sixteenth century. Here the ultimate focus of mystery is Holy Nothingness, No-Thing-Ness, the undifferentiated, transcending indefinite from which all concrete manifestations emerge and to which they return. But the sense of an infinite indefiniteness is far more pervasive, and appears also quite apart from any reliance upon a religious or ontological tradition. In fact, the whole thesis that the modern world is secular and has lost the sacred needs to be strongly qualified by seeing that the sense of mystery before the indefinite is a widely present modern phenomenon, often not recognized either by its authors or those who respond to them as an expression of wonder, often inarticulate or despairing but nonetheless significant as one of the central expressions of the sense of wonder in our time. Modern writers have explored all the available avenues to try to show that life is lived without moorings, that it has no unity, and that it simply is what it is, unrelated to any setting or framework of meaning. But the background of such a vision is the indefinite or chaotic disorder out of which and against which life is lived, and it is in this background that mystery resides. Thus Nathan Scott comments on a group of French writers:

"The tradition, in other words, that extends from the great *poètes maudits* of the mid-nineteenth century through Mallarmé and Valéry to Pierre Reverdy and the Surrealists André Breton and Louis Aragon is a tradition on whose aim it has been to liberate the mind from the fragmentation and illusoriness of reality, in order that it might somehow gain an entry into the dark and primitive depths of Being itself: its goal is that cosmic point where all the scattered leaves of life are into one volume bound, where substance and accidents, and their modes, are all fused together into one blazing flame. . . . And in his *Second Manifeste,* André Breton declared: 'Everything suggests the belief that there is a certain point of the mind where life and death, the real and the imaginary, the past and the future, the communicable and the incommunicable, the high and the low are no longer perceived as contradictions. It would be vain to look for any motive in surrealist activity other than the hope of determining that point.'" [1]

It proved most difficult to bring to expression the vision of the infinite point of unity, where there are no more contrasts between life and death, past and future; and the later history of this French tradition has been the story of a literature of despair rather than of hope, and a story that is almost entirely devoid of anything that we can recognize as sacred or wonderful. But whether one looks at the intricate, indefinitely extended detail of surface in Robbe-Grillet, or at the unbearably extended description of detail in Beckett's novels, it is not amiss to see here a negative, or perhaps shadow, form of the infinite. The definite (and in both writers mentioned, as in Kafka, definite detail is of the essence of their style) has ceased to be related to anything, so that the infinite reappears in the form of the indefinite totality, a totality of zero. Modern literature is full, as Beckett says of the things that happen to Watt, of "incidents of great formal brilliance and of indeterminable purport," incidents of which it can be said "that a thing that was nothing had happened, with the utmost formal distinctness." [2] The pervasive sense of an indefinite infinity as the backdrop against which the fragmentary concrete appears comes to expression not only in one line of literary development but very widely in recent literature. It would be foolish to "baptize" it into the circle of the negative sacred of Buddhism or Isaac Luria. But it would be equally foolish to pass over the lure of the indefinite, the desolate, unending unrelated expanse that is the only mystery still perceptible to so many today. There may be a hint in its very infinity that this indefiniteness is somehow "commanding."

At any rate it is clear that the shift from infinity conceived as the infinite extension of known qualities to the infinity of indefiniteness has not been a shift conducive to hope. For hope, despite its unpredictable character, thrives when it has a "place," and the lack of place for man and his world is the central thrust of this whole wing of modern sensibility. Yet the complexity of the situation and the vigor of at least some remnants of hope can be seen in the very persistence of the beaten-down protagonists in these works. Thus, Beckett can be treated as a writer of pure despair, a man with a vision that not only begins but stays at zero, as he is interpreted in the brilliant essay of Nathan Scott cited above. But this view overlooks the stubborn way in which the figures carry on in his stories, despite their lack of place. And Beckett himself, apparently, puts a high value on this second reading of his work.

Does the imagination, cut loose from the infinite on which it was brought up by Western Christianity, have to remain on the zero point, the dead center of a world infinitely random and indefinite? One way forward is to give indefiniteness the ultimate meaning of the primordial reality, and we noted above that this is often done by drawing on Eastern forms of understanding. We may expect further fruitful explorations of this theme. Another solution is to grasp this dark situation in an eschatological framework, and view it as the dawning of a total reversal, a view to which we now turn.

THE INFINITE AS THE END

No one has worked more seriously at conceiving the infinite or totality as the End than Thomas J. J. Altizer, and we refer to his work here rather than to Wolfhart Pannenberg or others who are more familiar as theologians of the End because Altizer's work is directed specifically at the situation that we have sketched above, a situation in which the significance of the concrete tends to be absorbed into one or another form of indefiniteness. Directly sensed as a situation of loss of meaning, this radical unsettling of all perspectives is given a reverse significance by Altizer through the theme "Descent into hell." [3] Drawing on the eschatological tradition that we shall examine later, Altizer holds that total redemption takes place through total reversal, and a key feature of this reversal will be (or, is, to the extent that it is already real) the loss both of personal identity and (for the Christian) of all sense of the particular identity of the Christian faith. Transcendence is here associated with form and hence with repression, and the movement toward the future is a movement toward radical, total immanence. Altizer has much in common with those who try to give meaning to the experience of alienation, disorientation, and loss of transcendence by returning to a primordial, undifferentiated infinity, as it is known in Eastern religion. But this Eastern vision, in its usual form, he sees as a return to the beginning and therefore a flight from history, rather than as an acceptance of history and a movement into the future. The West, with its sense of the Fall and history, must be brought together with the East and its sense of the primordial undifferentiated infinity. They can be brought together, Altizer holds, by viewing history in a radically Hegelian-apocalyptic manner in which the Western structural pattern is given Eastern content. The Buddhist nirvana reflects the pre-Fall undifferentiated unity which the West can no longer experience. And the End will be, not a return to this beginning but nonetheless an embodiment of a movement out of it which includes it in a new form. The End is radical, total immanence which not only leaves behind the transcendent God who has come to function as repression, but also leaves behind the separate centers of consciousness which have been so grotesquely exaggerated in the Western style of consciousness.

Much of this may sound quite gnostic to some readers, but Altizer is striving precisely to reverse the gnostic flight from this world to a higher reality. "Just as Buddhist love is unreal if it appears by way of the actuality and reality of the world," he remarks, "so Christian love is unreal if it appears apart from the brute reality of the full historical actuality of a fallen world." [4] Further, in contrast to a widely held view, Altizer says that love is not acceptance of the other. It is rather an attack upon all distance that creates and also alienates the other, an attack upon the estrangement of a fallen condition. This eschatological love can only be named Christ and is actually the reality of Christ.

In this serious and powerful vision we have an attempt to pass directly into and through the infinity of indefiniteness that has reappeared in the modern world and has replaced the infinity of experienced quality. There is no returning to the old God who had infinite but definite qualities of goodness and power! For he is known to be repressive—Altizer has this in common with the sensibility that has rediscovered the indefinite infinity. But unlike most of the spokesmen for that insight, he resists the motif of return that makes the indefinite meaningful or bearable to men such as Richard Rubenstein, Alan Watts, or Norman O. Brown, all of whom view the indefinite through the experiences of Western or Eastern mysticism. The dawn of meaning in the abyss of vagueness cannot take place through a movement backward. There must be a resolute motion forward, and to this motion corresponds the symbol of the End as total redemption. The End will be an inversion or total reversal of the undifferentiated point of origin, and will at the same time be a total coincidence of opposites. In Hegelian terms, it will be the complete passing of Spirit in itself (transcendent Spirit) into Spirit for itself (immanent Spirit). This reality cannot be known or confronted by flight from history.

This perspective takes with utmost seriousness the need for bringing into coherence the deepest insights of East and West. It is not accidental that Altizer's thought has been deeply stimulated by Orthodox Christianity, which is more open to a theology of the Spirit than is the thought of the West. The effort to bring together East and West, Buddhism and Christianity, must be a prime concern of theology for a long time to come. But it appears that at the present time a resolution is premature. The faiths of the East must be recognized as expressing an encounter with ultimate reality as profound as that of the West. But the two perspectives, for the present at least, in the last analysis offer a choice rather than the possibility of a synthesis. At any rate this is the case from the perspective of this book. Why this is so will become apparent as we make a further examination of the concept of infinity.

In Altizer's thought the concept of infinity appears in the form of the infinite or total End, and the End means the breaking down of all barriers of consciousness, and the union of all consciousness in total immanence. His emphasis on process, and on God's involvement in process, is surely to be welcomed. His focus on love as total loss of distance is more questionable. Taking Christ as his central symbol, Altizer argues astutely from the New Testament as a starting point for his

concept of love as total mutual immanence. The questionable
thing is precisely the adjective "total." We can illustrate from
a powerful vision which makes concrete what seems to be the
central thrust of Altizer's vision of loss of distance and of total
mutual immanence. John Woolman, the eighteenth-century
New Jersey Quaker, records in his journal that at a time when
he was about fifty years old he was so sick that he became de-
lirious and could no longer remember his name. "Being then
desirous to know who I was, I saw a mass of matter of a dull
gloomy color to the South and East and was informed that this
mass was human beings in as great misery as they could be,
and live, and that I was mixed up with them, and henceforth I
might not consider myself as a distinct or separate being."
Later he hears an angelic voice, "John Woolman is dead." [5]
The interpretation is that he is united with the slaves digging
silver in the mines of South America, and his death is the
death of his own will. Here is a magnificent expression of the
death symbolism so central to Altizer, signifying for Woolman
as it does for him the breakdown of barriers between selves
("I might not consider myself a distinct or separate being").
But can this moment bear the weight of the totality of the
End? In Woolman's case he got well and resolved to abstain
from the use of silver as a testimony against this suffering with
which he found himself united. He resumed his separate focus
of existence but with a difference resulting from the momentary interpenetration and loss of distance. It cannot be otherwise. No moment can bear the weight of the "all" or be transformed into the all. For differentiation is of the essence of the
real. The End considered as an infinite totality, as we shall see
in our discussion of eschatology, is an unstable symbol for precisely this reason; the End symbolizes other things as well as a
total or infinite unity. Thus it is questionable whether the
effort of Altizer succeeds in making clear a vision fundamentally distinct from the vision of return to the undifferentiated
point of beginning which he is striving to go beyond. A vision
of the End which does go beyond the undifferentiated will
have to make place for some continuing form of distinction, of

differentiation. Altizer makes a real effort to uncover a form of faith that will have room for hope, but he does not succeed in clarifying how the End will differ from the primordial beginning.

A Process View of Infinity

Clearly, infinity is in the most powerful sense of the term an attractive concept. In different forms it appears as a central or often the central symbol of the ultimate mystery, or God. But each form in which infinity appears as a total, all-encompassing reality presents insuperable difficulties. If God is infinite in the sense that he is the infinite extension of qualities we experience as good, then he is forced into a competition with man which destroys either one or the other. If God is the indefinite infinity of the undifferentiated primordial beginning, he reduces the concrete experiences and moments of life to unreality. If God (or in Altizer's language, Christ) is the total End, then if this can be clarified to be different from the beginning, no other conceptuality than the old tradition of negative theology is open to give it meaning, and the attempt to speak in this way brings in elements which are meaningful as parts of reality but not as the whole, such as the interpretation of love as total loss of distance, which is meaningful only as part of the whole act of love.

Perhaps what is needed is a fresh view of infinity as a religious concept. If we take a pluralistic point of view, we shall be prepared to hold that there simply *is* no one all-satisfying, unifying all. There is no such reality as an all-comprehending infinity in the sense of the indefinite infinity or the infinite End. The infinity of experienced qualities, despite its rigidities, pointed in the right direction in holding that there are differentiations even in what is infinite. God cannot be all in all, since in the nature of things, God is only one of several fundamentally real entities.

Hence a process view of infinity as a religious concept must sort out three functions that have usually been confused: the infinity of possibility (the primordial nature of God); the total unification of reality (the consequent nature of God), and finally, the infinity which was so troublesome to the traditional Christian view, the infinity of perfection of quality. These three are quite distinct; each has a contribution to make to the way in which we are grasped by wonder at God and the world. The pluralistic view, that other realities are just as real as God, is a salutary and liberating antidote to the lure of the all-encompassing infinity or totality. This pluralistic view, as will appear, is much more congenial to hope than any of the other views.

The location of the indefinite infinite, in a process system, is the primordial nature of God. This is the realm of potentiality, the realm of possibilities—"eternal objects," as Whitehead calls them. On the principle that everything, even the unimaginably infinite range of possibilities, must be somewhere, Whitehead posits that possibilities as they become actualized in occasions do not come from nowhere but are offered to the occasion by God from the infinite store of possibilities in his primordial nature. This function of God, of course, is by no means an exclusively "religious" one; quite to the contrary, all occasions whatever stand in this relation to God's primordial nature, which is a presupposition required to understand the fact that possibilities do not become actual in a merely random way. But the very vastness and inexhaustibility of God's infinite store of possibilities may become the focus of awe, an awe that is fundamentally the same as the awe of the archaic or Eastern man before the primordial undifferentiated infinite.

But there is a difference. For the primordial nature of God as the locus of infinite possibility is not undifferentiated. Interpreters of Whitehead differ on the question of how much ranking or ordering of the possibilities is implied by the fact that all are unified in God's primordial valuation of them.[6] But at any rate it is fundamental to a process perspective that possibilities are not just random, appearing from the infinite and receding into it again. The store of possibilities is the well of novelty rather than the merely undifferentiated ground of being. This can be so, for one thing, because the primordial nature of God is not "all." It functions in relation to other equally real entities, and thus does not swallow up reality as the archaic primordial reality does. The very term "primordial" is misleading to those whose vocabulary is shaped by the archaic image. For an ordered range of possibilities (coming to actuality by reason of their relevance to what now is, rather than just randomly) is a central basis of the lure toward real novelty which is so much a part of the now frustrated intuition of our culture, and which is also a central aspect of Whitehead's view of process.

The Whiteheadian perspective makes possible a shift of imaginative focus from a past-oriented primordial undifferentiated totality to a future-oriented realm of unexplored possibilities which come into actuality by reason of their potential of carrying forward the movement to novelty which is actually under way. The lure of the unknown, the lure of the infinite that is not yet, and the lure that the finite moment move beyond itself can all be brought together as the transformation of the archaic lure of the undifferentiated infinite. The primordial nature of God is oriented to the new rather than to the "primordial" in the archaic sense. Thus infinite possibility does not require us to accept a pattern of eternal recurrence or the higher reality of undifferentiated being.

The second aspect of the infinite, the infinite or total unification of reality, is closely related to the first, but, at least as we analyze our experience, it requires to be separated from it. We have to keep on seeing that the older intuition is trustworthy, namely, that there is an infinitely extended unification of reality in God, but we need to learn that God's unification of reality is not a once-for-all totality whether of primordial beginning or final end. Again we touch on the realism of the process perspective, here in respect to time. However deeply shaped time is by our perception of it, time is nonetheless utterly real, and the unification of all things in God is enriched by or if you will, subject to, time. In other words, infinite unification takes place moment by moment, and does not endure; the totality of

God's realization is a serially enriched totality and not a static one. It is something of a puzzle that Western thought has resisted this notion for so long; of course it did so in the name of the eminence or greatness of God. "God is all-sufficient unto himself," in the words of the confession cited at the beginning of this chapter. On a process view he is not all-sufficient unto himself, but essentially related to all things. His relatedness is what makes it possible to think of God as a focus of unification.

At this point in rethinking the meaning of infinity we are deeply indebted to Charles Hartshorne, who has seen, perhaps more clearly than any other thinker, the inherent conflict within the concept of infinity with which this chapter started, and who has developed, in the name of surrelativism or panentheism, a concept of God as the *most* related entity, whose concrete relatedness embraces his abstract absoluteness.[7] Hartshorne's phrase for the cumulative, successively enriched infinity is "the self-surpassing surpasser of all." Looking at the question from the angle of perfection and absoluteness rather than infinity, he shows that a God understood as self-surpassing is more perfect than an absolute, unrelated, impassible God. Against the static notion of God's infinite unification, he remarks, "the totality of changes can very well change, by the addition of new changes, previously inactualized." [8]

Time is elusive at best, and there are real obstacles in the view of God as the ever-present unifying point of cumulative reality. Those who wish to follow this point further may read the criticism of Hartshorne by John T. Wilcox, based on time's relativity to standpoint, and the reply by Lewis S. Ford.[9] We leave this problem aside to concentrate on the meaning of this "panentheist" viewpoint for the response of wonder, for we believe that such a cumulatively enriched infinity can provide just that dislocation of the imagination required to allow wonder to enter the multifarious world that so many find depressing. Quite to the contrary of many who find that the absence of a final end in a process view deprives God of the greatness that merits a religious response, we find that the view of God as forward-moving and ever-enriched can become the focus of a renewed sense of wonder, precisely because it makes the unity that religious intuition seeks concrete (if passing) rather than abstract.

Finally, we return to the form of infinity which was central in earlier Western imagination: the infinite extension of known and valued qualities, God as infinitely good. Such an affirmation is essential to faith. Yet in its earlier form it became so threatening that it forced the whole image of God out of consciousness. But once we accept the consequence of a process view, that God is one entity among others, and essentially involved in time and relatedness (God is, in other words, in some respects limited in comparison with the older theism), then the intuition of God's infinite completion of qualities we know and value ceases to be threatening and becomes liberating. Despite the fact that the forms of thought are entirely different, there is a real point of contact here with early Christianity and with some aspects of the contemporary theology of secularization. For the presence of God in suffering, and the suffering of God for and with the world become comprehensible as they never could in the days of the "impassible" God. As Hartshorne finely says, those who suffer are not "mere external products of an impassive first cause, but integral members of the all sensitive passive aspect or 'consequent nature' of the divine, who suffers in and through all their suffering." [10]

To summarize, Christianity (or Judaism and Christianity, more accurately) introduced into the West an understanding of infinity as not simply indefinite but as a concrete infinity of valued qualities: infinite goodness, holiness, etc. This shift in the image of infinity was the correlative of a shift which made hope a central religious response, because the believer found that his concrete existence was of real meaning to God himself. But this insight combined with the absoluteness and transcendence of God showed itself, in the course of many centuries of experience with it, to be a kind of infinity threatening to man. God's infinite qualities did not leave any room for man to function with dignity. The result has been, either in a mood of despair or one of tranquillity, a shift back again to the infinite as the indefinite on the part of a large segment of sensitive modern people. But if we can so dislocate our imaginations as to break up the image of infinity into three aspects: the infinity of possibility, the concrete infinity of the unity of the moment in God, and the infinite goodness of the related rather than absolute God, there will still be room for the distinctive contribution of the Christian vision, the infinite extension of the concrete qualities known to be best. This dislocation does mean giving up the idea that God is wholly transcendent and self-sufficient. Some think that a God so related to the world is unworthy of awe and wonder, but to the contrary we hold that this perspective will liberate awe and wonder, and hope as well. The alternative route, to return to the archaic sense of the indefinite infinite, is appealing because it draws on ancient perceptions and ancient emotional patterns.

We revert to our symbol from the first chapter, the child. Both the stance of hope arising from the freedom of the process perspective and the stance of return to the archaic can be illuminated by this symbol of the child: hope by the child as a symbol of the forward movement of life; the return to the undifferentiated by the adult looking back at the child's world and longing to return to it, or through it to the undifferentiated state that preceded it. Difficult as it is to envision the dismantling and restructuring of the imagination that we call for, and cautious as we must be since there are as yet few signs of response to this vision on the part of men with creative imagination, we nonetheless present this tripartite view of the infinite as profoundly hopeful and liberating. Perhaps it is not too much to suppose that, since the contemporary imagination is largely shaped by possibilities worked out by such men as Hume, Kant, and Hegel, we should not despair that the impact of such men as Whitehead and Hartshorne is not yet great.

Finally, we can relate the response of hope, seen in a process framework, to the structure of experience more clearly. We return again to the two modes of apprehending a mysterious "beyond": the mode of ecstasy, in which time seems suspended, and the mode of hope, in which a future fulfillment is expected. Though each of these is a macroscopic experience, each can be understood from a process point of view as an accentuation of an aspect of the moment of concrescence which is the ultimate unit of experience. Each occasion, viewed from the outside, is an indivisible "droplet" of experience that cannot be analyzed into successive parts. Yet each occasion has an internal structure which we can understand only in terms of primary and supplementary aspects. The final aspect of an actual occasion is its "satisfaction," in which all the elements are unified. It is by stressing the character of an occasion of experience as a movement toward unification in satisfaction that one is led to the primacy of ecstasy or disorientation to time. Here infinity is glimpsed through the dissolution of the links that bind one occasion to another. Such moments represent an immense heightening of the valuation placed upon the occasion of experience, a recognition that its limited unification of the reality available to it is analogous to God's unification of reality. For this reason, there is a tendency to cling to such moments and to imagine that their indefinite prolongation would be the ultimate fulfillment.

Another aspect of the actual occasion is its dynamic character of aiming at a goal. Whitehead was right in seeing that the internal goal of an occasion is not wholly isolated from its expected future. An occasion aims at a satisfaction that will prepare the way for as full a realization as possible of the intensity it seeks in the relevant future as well. It is this aspect of subjective aim, subjective aim not only as functioning in a discrete moment but also reaching toward its relevant future, that supplies the clue to the reach toward infinity in the future. But this is a different kind of infinity, for it is a processive infinity without term. Of course, an aim toward the future does not have to be seen as related to infinite possibility.

Most purpose and hope is much more limited, and aims at a specific goal. The infinite possibility of time has in its full weight been a recent discovery in human culture, and it is still so new that we do not quite know what to make of it. Men were creative for centuries before they saw that truly creative action presses past the goal it starts with toward a beyond, and that the beyond always beckons, no matter how great the creative achievement. Our dramatic sense shapes events into stories that come to an end, and this sense also expresses a profound truth that must be taken account of. Yet each end turns out to be a new beginning as well.

There are therefore two possibilities for centering experience: the occasion as a detached satisfaction, or the occasion as dynamic and reaching toward a goal. Both have played a role in faith. The former moment has a longer history in religion, while at least in Western history faith has brought the latter more into its consciousness. However varied the evaluation of the Judeo-Christian tradition may be, it would be hard to avoid the conclusion that it has been the principal source of this greater awareness of the dynamic of action and hope toward the future. At the present moment, however, our culture and faith are in reaction against this second emphasis because it came to expression in the rigid form of divine determination of the end. But another reason for this recoil is the difficulty and newness of the notion of infinitely enriched infinity. From the days of archaic religion, with its eternal repetition of what the gods did in the beginning, to the rediscovery of eternal recurrence by Schopenhauer and Nietzsche, the alternative to a goal predetermined by an absolute deity has usually seemed to be the repetition of a limited set of possibilities. One of the immense merits of the White-headian perspective is that it clearly offers a third alternative to what has so often seemed to be the only two choices. This third alternative can provide a new "house" for hope, which is no longer at home in the rigid structure of the predetermined end.

Part Two
HOPE
AND CHRISTIAN FAITH

IV
Secularization

The first three chapters showed that a relevant setting in which hope can live—a "house for hope"—can better be afforded by a theology of process than by the other options that are of broad appeal today. Now we begin to ask more directly whether such a theology of process can make *Christian* hope meaningful; can it stand in a relation of fulfillment to the forms of hope that are central for Christians?

We begin at the most controversial point: the question of God and religion. The first section of this book has shown that an assault on that current sensibility which blocks out all awareness of God need not be a retreat to the past, but on the contrary can open the way toward a future in which man and world can be related to each other in a meaningful way. The movement called "theology of secularization" has been working with a directly Christian perspective toward the same end, to bring man into a real and responsible relation to his world. But it has done so, like so much of the purely secular sensibility, largely by setting aside the question of God, for the traditional God seemed to belong in a separate realm, a higher world that has become unreal.

Secularization in the sense of turning away from a separate realm of God and religion is obvious enough. But secularization is not only a fact; it is widely hailed as both a product of Christian faith and as a liberating process for Christian faith. Hope and secularization go hand in hand in the theologies of today. Not only do the theologies of hope strongly emphasize the worldliness of Christianity, but the theologies in which secularization is a central term stress the reality of hope. In all this writing, secularization is not always very clearly defined, but in any case it means a movement away from a separate realm of God and religion toward the world where things "really happen." To make clear the relation of a Christian process theology to secularization, we must bring the views of the first three chapters into dialogue with the Christian tradition.

Insofar as theologies of secularization accept the modern movement away from God, it is the God of infinite power who is rejected. Thus secularization is an expression of the same rebellion against an outmoded view of infinity that was discussed in Chapter III. Against the predestinarian-determining view of God, a recent theologian says forthrightly that "unless we make it be, the Kingdom of God shall never come. . . . In a word, there is no 'divine plan.' " [1] Dietrich Bonhoeffer, the most quoted author on the theme of secularization, points in the same direction of human assumption of responsibility with his phrase "man come of age," meaning a man who no longer has to depend on God to do for him what he is to do himself.

Insofar as the emphasis in secularization is on the movement away from religion, it is religion as a separate higher sphere of man's activity and awareness that is rejected. The "sacred" appears to be the static, the rigidly ritual, indeed the realm of pious generality apart from the concrete acts that constitute existence. Thus the theologies of secularization are not at all friendly to those movements of recovery of archaic religion and the primordial sacred which are a striking feature of culture in America today. Writers on secularization see the claim of the sacred as "totality," which we have noticed, and reject this lure of totality as essentially static. The sacred, they hold, detaches man from concrete involvement in history.

Rather than to religion or to the sacred, the theologies of secularization want to turn man toward living in the social world of the fellowman where responsibility and freedom are really exercised.

These aspects of secularization are highly congenial to a Christian process theology which, as we have seen, is also reacting against the absolute God of infinite power and against the sacred totality that dissolves the multifarious pluralism of actual existence. At the same time, the previous chapter has shown that the rejection of a wrong notion of infinity does not have to lead to a rejection either of God or of infinity as a religious reality. Though a process theology will be extremely sympathetic to the theologies of secularization, it must ask whether much in these theologies is not based on precisely the idea of God which we now see is outmoded. There is a much closer interaction between God and man (or self) than such theologies seem to think when they concentrate so sharply on the problems of man alone. This one-sidedness becomes evident when we note that all of the important writers on the theology of secularization presuppose that free and responsible action in faith is possible. But outside of the theological circle, the very coherence of the responsible self is thought of as eroding away. In its attempt to be rid of the religious dimension, the theology of secularization is losing the framework that best provides the chance to recover a coherent and responsible self.

BACKGROUND

First, a word about background. In the European Protestant vocabulary, religion has been a "bad" word for a long time, mainly because religion was thought of as man's performance before God. The strong emphasis on man's receptivity before God, or on justification by faith, in this tradition, led it to try to exclude all thought of human achievement. In coining the phrase "non-religious interpretation of Christian faith," Bonhoeffer was bringing to the very center of his theological effort a usage of words that was already familiar in his tradition.

In the United States, on the other hand, religion has been a positive word both in the popular and in the theological vocabulary, and it remains so today. This favorable use of the word originated in a strongly Christ-centered Puritan piety, but it later broadened into a more general use, especially under the influence of the trend toward deism. Gradually a kind of American secular religion has developed which is too much ignored by theologians. Partly it is raw, unreflective nationalism; it contains elements of the older belief in progress; but it has also absorbed from its Puritan origin and from Christian liberalism some sense of the possibility of prophetic judgment upon itself. Thus this civic religion, for all its defensiveness and naïveté, has some contact with a view of religion as that which stands over against culture and judges it. The sense of movement to the future in American popular religion is not wholly one of self-aggrandizement and American destiny. The "prophetic" element of criticism has been able to remain in some kind of dialogue with this secularized religion of American culture. This was true in the days of Walter Rauschenbusch, the great spokesman for the "social gospel"; it has been true of Reinhold Niebuhr, who interpreted the social history of the depression and the Second World War to a much wider audience than the churches; and it remains true today of the theologians of secularization, who are in constant dialogue with nontheological partners.

In contrast, the European liberal theology (despite the Christian Socialists and men such as Leonhard Ragaz) was more romantic and was less able to enter into critical dialogue with its culture. The result has been that in the United States theologians have been very reluctant to separate the power of God or Christ from the cultural context as the main wing of Protestant European thinking has done. The Americans have thought that the power they were trying to clarify was at work at least in a diffuse way through the culture; the Europeans

were trying to emphasize the radical transcendence of faith
over culture. That in the United States we still use "religion"
as a positive term springs from this different background. The
result is that the negative judgment on "religion" in American
theology is not so thoroughgoing as that of our European
counterparts, despite the similarity of much that is written
about secularization.

It would be easy to conclude that in this question as in so
many others, Americans are now only just catching up to Eu-
rope and recognizing how empty of hope their culture is. This
widespread reading of the present crisis contains a real measure of truth. There is no doubt that many American churches
and theologians retained—in spite of Reinhold Niebuhr,
whose realistic view of human nature is hard for many students of today to take—an unwarranted degree of naïve optimism and a too-easy identification with hopeful and forward-
looking elements in our culture. But this is not the whole
story. American theologians, some of them at least, have seen
as clearly as any others the extent to which religion is a cultural product. Yet they have tended to believe that the religious phenomenon could be "saved," that under the influence
of elements in American religion, both churchly and secular,
men could listen to prophetic criticism and recognize themselves and their culture as standing under judgment. The
choice between these two valuations of the cultural scene does
not depend on some general theological principle, but on the
actual condition of the culture: How apt is it to express a
movement toward what can be trusted? There is a widespread
conviction that the popular religion of America has become essentially backward-looking and therefore can have no meaning for a future-oriented theology of hope.

We have come a long way from the vision that Walter
Rauschenbusch expressed with power in his book of 1907,
Christianity and the Social Crisis, in one chapter of which he
examined the reasons why Christianity had never undertaken
the work of social reconstruction, and concluded that these

reasons were ceasing to be operative. We recognize the irony of the American dream of a new world. Yet at the same time one can remain in this American tradition as a theologian of today. We have exchanged a confident belief in progress for an awareness of the open and precarious nature of historical change. But that does not mean that we have simply to cultivate a sense of the essential intractability of things. I for one believe that the sober theologian of today can stand affirmatively in this American tradition at the same time that he stands critically in it. The easy overlay of faith and American destiny is something that we are well rid of, and also the earlier uncritical optimism. But the emphasis on God's presence in the actual world of man and society is still to be affirmed. So is the insight that faith and culture are in constant interplay, so that the ultimate mystery is mediated not only by "proclamation," but by sex, creativeness, work, human interaction, and by the widest reaches of the imagination as well as by easily recognizable Christian channels. Such a perspective will blur the distinction between faith and religion, between Christian and non-Christian, and this has the advantage of corresponding to the facts in a way that a radical disjunction between faith and culture cannot do.

Here we find the difference between the present time and earlier ways of thinking about how the distinctively Christian tradition lives and expresses itself. In earlier times one could say that a recognizable community, the church, was the locus of this kind of life. This is presupposed in the New Testament. But this is no longer the case. The church cannot think of itself as the exclusive place where the realities it knows are known. However, in marked contrast to a widespread trend among theologians of secularization, we conclude from this that the church is in the process of discovering for itself a new and vital role. It is to be the place where a community clarifies and toughens the claim of the Christian style of life, and this role is all the more essential because of the threat of diffusion and loss in the pluralistic situation. To discern the kind of humanness that is compatible with a Christian life-style, to affirm it whether or not it understands itself as an expression of faith, and to provide a center within which the fundamental bases of the Christian life-style can be uncovered and reflected upon: these are pressing tasks, which are not to be by-passed in favor of simple humanness in the world. For humanness is not that simple, and while the Christian style of life is not the only authentic and caring way to be human, it is, we believe, all too probable that the emerging post-Christian possibilities may really be sub-Christian.

LEVELS OF SECULARIZATION

The religious dimension which is eroded by secularization can be analyzed into three levels. First, the sacred as that which impels wonder, as the mystery "beyond and within" what is encountered in experience. Second, the sacred as the ultimate ordering factor in the cosmos, that which precisely makes the cosmos a cosmos; more graphically, this aspect of the sacred may be called the "sacred canopy," to use Peter Berger's expression, which overarches the world.[2] The doctrine of creation expresses this relation to the world in Christianity. Third, the sacred as organized into institutions through which its superiority over the profane may be exercised. In any society that is traditionally religious, these aspects of the sacred are actually met in reverse order, of course. The sacred is most obviously known in its concrete expression in cult, sacred law, custom, and "church" or religious institutions or in the religious dimension of the institutions of society generally. An intellectual elite may speak theologically or philosophically of the second level, the sacred as an ordering factor, but in any case this phase will come to expression in myth. The first aspect, the most general dimension of awe and wonder, will not find any expression apart from myth and cult. Awareness of it as something separable belongs to a relatively sophisticated and reflective stage of culture. But as has been shown in the previous chapter, awareness of awe and wonder does still appear apart from any sense of cosmos or "sacred canopy," even in the most "desacralized" world. This fact should lead us to be careful about affirming that modern men live in a totally desacralized world. Even many who think that they do will rediscover the sense of ultimate mystery as we have shown in discussing the "indefinite infinite."

It is clear that the process of secularization works backward through the series also. Secularization is first manifest as the process whereby the institutions of society are freed from religious control. Indeed, Berger defines secularization as "the process by which sections of society and culture are removed from the domination of religious institutions and symbols." [3] The breakup of the traditional institutional functions of the sacred contributes to making manifest the erosion of the "sacred canopy," the ordering of the world by religious symbols, and tends to thrust the religious dimension into the realm of private and inward experience. In this respect pietistic Protestantism, like existentialism, is a fruit of secularization. Both renounce a vision of the whole in favor of the intensity of a particular internal fragment. Finally, the sense of awe or wonder will become problematic, despite the fact that it is much more persistent than first appears.

It is probably true that the sense of wonder is most thoroughly eliminated from areas longest exposed to secularization. The economic life is more secularized than the inner life or the political life, or, for that matter, the military life. If a leader of industry is murdered, his death does not acquire symbolic significance, while the religious significance of the death of political figures is clear enough. Again, economic life has no symbol like the flag. Military affairs, by contrast, are very imperfectly secularized, in large part because of their close connection with death.

As the institutional forms of the sacred collapse the areas freed from control undergo a process of rationalization. Economics again offers the obvious illustration; it is the most mathematical of the social sciences.

But this "rationalization" is not nearly so rational a process as its name implies. It is rational to the extent that it means applying pragmatic and managerial techniques to the securing of widely desired aims, instead of submitting to a given and sacred tradition. To stay with the economic illustration, it is clear that the aims of Western technology are indeed widely desired. The apparently inexorable attractiveness of this technology in all human cultures is a key to the revolutionary changes taking place in the world today. The real center of the nonrationality of the "rationalization" which goes on when the sacred recedes does not lie in the fact that secularization and the technological rationalization of a society do not actually achieve for the society as a whole the economic hopes which attract people to the process. But this frustrating experience of all technologically developed societies does point to the real issue. Technology shapes all aspects of life, and transforms culture profoundly, but it does not supply its own direction. In our affluent society we are seldom aware of the pressure of the economic aims that make men consent to industrial and social management, but despite this pressure, these economic and technological processes are not self-directing.

We can see this clearly when a new perspective is forced upon us. The ecological limitations on technology are forcing a complete rethinking of modern expansionist economics. And —important to note!—the ecological literature is full of a sense of wonder. The very area that has been most thoroughly secularized and rationalized is finding new direction, not from the old static and authoritative sacred, but nonetheless from a sense of wonder and respect for the world which has its own integrity and also makes human life possible. We may cite the motif of the "endangered species." Some of these species, like the California condor, are types for which we cannot feel much empathy, but one cannot read what is written about endangered species without sensing the reverence before the wonderfully involved and precariously self-maintaining structures of life. In a very different setting from the unpatterned vagueness of the indefinite infinite, we run against the power of an ultimate mystery, and this mystery has something very concrete to do with the reshaping of technological and empirical goals.

Certainly there is no prospect for a return to a society in which religious institutions exercise a controlling role. Small and very diverse segments within modern society will reaffirm this ancient style of life, but all the prospects are that such disciplined groups will remain small and varied. Few will opt for them. In this sense secularization is an irreversible process, at least for our foreseeable future. Thus the pluralism of society and the diffuse appearance of the response of awe and wonder in it does not merely require that those who are committed to a Christian style of life turn toward being responsible in the world. It also requires that they seek to find ways of newly grasping the dimension of wonder and awe, and that they be able to relate the general and vague intimations of wonder which we see around us to the specific focus of wonder from which Christian faith arises. If these tasks can be achieved, the movement of faith into the world can take place, not without risk of failure, but with a knowledge of how faith fits into the world to which it reaches out.

THE SACRED AS AN ORDERING FACTOR

If we notice that symbolic mystery still functions in many aspects of our pluralistic and seemingly secularized society, we shall see the need of being clearer about the second level of the earlier traditional manifestation of the sacred: the "sacred canopy," or ultimate ordering factor in a cosmos. Since the time of the pre-Socratic philosophers, thought has been separating the ordering factor from the sacred, as an expression of the freedom of thought against the static character of the archaic sacred. Nevertheless, the relation between a vision of a sacred cosmos and a vision of a cosmos ordered in some nonsacred way is not a simple one. The pre-Socratic philosophers themselves can be seen either as breaking the sacred reality or as continuing to work with respect for the ultimate mystery. For myself, I would see a thread of wonder and awe in the whole history of Western philosophy down to the present time, and would concur with Teilhard de Chardin that research is closer than it knows to adoration.[4] But the whole story can be viewed from the other side, as a struggle to free the mind from the confining and vague forms of sacred myth or authoritative theology, an effort initiated by the pre-Socratics and brought to completion by modern positivistic thought. The correct element in this interpretation is that the static and authoritarian character of the archaic sacred has been decisively overthrown. That religious wonder is thereby eliminated does not follow.

Rather than pursue the ramifications of this debate, however, it is more important for the subject of hope that we look at a development from it. This is the characteristically modern attempt to refrain from living in a cosmos at all. For many, the question of cosmos or ordered world does not appear as sacred cosmos versus secular order. Instead, existence and meaning are seen as so fragmented that there is no order at all. From this perspective, order, if it is allowed even psychological reality, is understood to be repressive, and the elimination of the sacred sanction of order is affirmed in the name of freedom. Frequently this characteristically secular perspective is taken up into the theologies of secularization. Harvey Cox, for instance, celebrated secularization as "the disenchantment of nature, the desacralization of politics, and the deconsecration of values," perspectives which he derived from the Old Testament, though he held that they reach effectiveness in American pragmatism and profanity.[5] Long before Cox, Friedrich Gogarten emphasized the advantage to faith in accepting the relativity and fragmentation of existence as modern men, not of course from a simply secular perspective but with the conviction that faith has its own kind of rootage which is not dependent on the old style of "sacred canopy." But if faith is as deeply interactive with cultural factors as we find it to be, the attempt to think of it separately from them is full of dangers. Only if the basis of faith can be clarified in relation to some kind of dependability also known elsewhere can the man of faith hope that his faith can genuinely interact with the whole world of experience.

Just as the pluralistic society calls for a thorough rethinking of the role of the religious institution, so the secularization of thought about order and the attempt to evade order altogether in understanding oneself call for a drastic rethinking of the sacred as an ordering factor. As has already been shown in analyzing the infinite, a reaction against a rigid and nonprocessive order does not at all require a rejection of order. The archaic models of the sacred are no longer viable, but the option of detaching all order from the ultimate mystery is equally unworkable. What we need is to recognize the partial and relative function of any specific way we have of understanding order, and at the same time to be aware of the way in which things continually reorder themselves whenever old orders are broken up. This will mean that order is not sacrosanct, as in the old "sacred canopy" way of perceiving it. Vast reaches of order can be grasped in a purely rational and secular way, and this is also true of aspects of God himself. But the function of order also reaches beyond what we can rationally grasp, and in particular the reach of processive historical order into the future brings us to the dimension of awe or wonder (either in hope or despair) that was once embodied in the archaic experience of the "sacred canopy."

ULTIMATE WONDER

So far as the first or most general dimension of the sacred is concerned, the sacred as that which impels awe or wonder, it requires a venturesome mind to try to see where we stand with respect to it. The archaic form of the sense of wonder is so worn away that Eliade can speak of a "second" fall of the awareness of the sacred into the unconscious.[6] There, we may add, it functions in an archetypal or past-oriented fashion. It may be the case that a style of existence has emerged, or will emerge, that will be wholly without a sense of awe or mystery. Yet I am impressed not only by the remnants of awe that we find both in the formal and the secular religion and also in the resurgence of archaic practices (astrology, witchcraft), but equally by the continuing quest for a clarification of the intimations of awe that open themselves to modern men in their ordinary existence: the mystery of human relations, of nature, of scientific insight. Further, we have mentioned the strange way in which the very lack of order and definition seems to be on the way to becoming a new sacred space for many. The very rebelliousness and negativity against traditional modes of acknowledging the wonderful often express a stubborn affirmation that "nevertheless" there is the wonderful in life. In a moment we shall try to reformulate this continuing sense of wonder in a way relevant, not to the static or primordial archaic sacred, but to the processive and historical world that we now perceive. Then it will become apparent that hope and awe are not antithetical, that the new vision of the sacred is one that is open and liberating of trust.

SECULARIZATION AND THE BIBLICAL TRADITION

Before we turn to a new vision of the wonderful, it is important for us to look briefly at the thesis that secularization is a principal fruit of Biblical faith. Harvey Cox made this a central theme of his *Secular City.* Many others have made the same point. Arend Th. van Leeuwen, in his *Christianity in World History,* has offered one of the most carefully argued statements of the case that Biblical faith is the end of religion, but the source of modern secular and technological society.[7] Van Leeuwen holds that the great ancient civilizations were ordered by a static and authoritarian concept of being, and that the linear, forward-moving, and secular style of civilization is a product of the faith in the Biblical God of history who shatters the static orders of being. The relation of his thesis to our discussion in the previous chapter is brought out in his analysis of the traditional Chinese state; he says it was "governed by a cosmic totality." [8] The unchanging nature, by definition, of totality, produced a frozen style of both government and religion. Consequently he argues that technology and industrialization which break up the sacred patterns are doing the work started by Biblical faith. Much of van Leeuwen's polemic is directed against the theology which was too blind to see this connection because too static itself. Thus he holds that the missionaries should have supported the Taiping rebellion of the 1850's against the Manchu dynasty, and that Mao's communism in important respects carries forward the necessary task of shattering the sacred structure of an outmoded archaic civilization, despite its retention of archaic totalitarian features.

There is much truth in this reading of history, the more so since it provides a healthful deflation of the "Christian ideology" which has identified the future of faith with the destiny of a particular civilization. But historical connections are not simple. The whole equation of historical-linear with technological-secular is too much of an oversimplification. The sources of science and technology were more in Greece than in the Bible, and regardless of the question of historical origin, we do not accept them because we take credit for their point of origin, but because we believe they can be turned to human uses.

We are on sounder ground to say that the general archaic pattern of perception saw change as a factor antithetical to the sacred. The sacred was understood as the power from which life was derived, not as a repressive power. But it was a source to which one returned perennially to cancel out change. The Biblical tradition, however, despite its variety, came to understand God as involved in change. Often the Biblical writers did not carry this insight very far, and the old style of "eternal return" makes itself felt in the Bible and in the development

of Christianity as well. Nonetheless, from a basic perspective
which saw men as struggling with the sacred or with God, the
Old Testament and the New develop a picture of the struggle
between God and man which sees God as so deeply involved
in the struggle that he cannot remain the remote and unchanging God of archaic religion. God is concerned for the *new* outcome, not just for a repetition of the original situation. A further deepening of this perspective, already present in the Old
Testament but particularly strong in the New Testament,
transforms the struggle to see God as the persuader rather
than as the one who compels. Even more: he suffers with and
in the world. These intuitions, that God is active in the course
of changing events, that he is involved and affected and even
suffers, and that he is finally not a determining force but a persuasive one, were never fully worked out in relation to the
older static notion of the sacred. The compromise that came
out in the course of a few centuries of Christian reflection on
the problem was the new concept of a God with infinitely extended qualities analogous to the human qualities of love and
power, a concept discussed in the previous chapter. Throughout the formative period, however, the immense majesty of
God's love and power was grasped in the fundamental context
of encounter or struggle, so that it was quickening rather than
repressive of human responsiveness and freedom.

The Biblical vision of a dynamic God in contest with man
and persuading man implies a profound restructuring of the
sacred. It is this restructuring which has to be carried through
if wonder and awe are to be other than marginal experiences.
The archaic pattern of return to the source of power and life
has tended to exalt the unchanging totality or infinity as that
which is most worthy of awe. This view was developed
beyond the archaic stage in the East, in Hinduism and Buddhism. There the changeless sacred implies the unreality of
the phenomenal world of change and calls men to realize the
wonder of the immediate but undifferentiated ultimate reality.
This formulation of the sacred has much appeal now in the

West for those who find the sense of wonder still an essential ingredient of human existence.

There is another alternative: to take even more seriously than the Biblical writers did, the involvement of God in time. It is an index of our resistance to this possibility that future-oriented faith still normally appears only in times of great tension, and as a vision of total and catastrophic change. If things are not too bad, the older style of return to the original pattern suffices, and it is only when existence is badly threatened that the direction of faith turns to the future, to the untried, as the locus of wonder and awe. This suggests that we need to learn a quite different style of vision if we are to rediscover the wonder which lures us into the future in good times as well as bad.

REIMAGINING THE SACRED AND GOD

Just as it turned out in trying to understand the infinite as a religious reality, so too the question of the sacred and secularization calls for a dramatic restructuring or skewing of our imagination and our thought. Here we must call upon both the resources of the Christian tradition and on process thought. They converge in their common concern with a dramatic, temporal view of existence and in their consequent distancing of themselves from the archaic sacred.

In process thought, God is not brought into the system in the first place as a sacred reality. Rather than the ineffable "beyond," God is so profoundly interactive with the world that neither can be understood without the other. Whitehead's provocative sentence might well be reflected on by those who think that secularization means focusing exclusively on the world: "The secularization of the concept of God's function in the world is at least as urgent a requisite of thought as is the secularization of other elements in experience." [9] Such a view will look on secularization quite differently from the usual

theologies of secularization which try to see how the man of
faith can live without God in the world (Bonhoeffer).

In the first place, a process view will make possible a fresh
approach to the whole question of order which has always
been so central in relation to the sacred. With God as part of a
processively ordered universe, it is possible to make sense of
both stability and the emergence of novelty. This way the
linear-historical sense of time in the Biblical tradition can be
brought into relation with the world of nature, which participates in the same processive order, instead of making history
essentially different from nature. Without God, the whole concept of process tends to break down into separate and unrelated moments (as consistently enough in some existentialist
views of history). The older Christian view of historical order,
the so-called sacred history view, held that God has established
a series of periods in history through the course of which his
purpose would be worked out. This view was able to think of
history as ordered by God's purpose. The deterministic side of
this older theory has by now all but destroyed it. The pattern
determined in advance was the historical counterpart of the
God of infinite power, who has been so widely rejected. But
the rigidity of this view need not mean that it should be rejected wholesale, for it comprehended the linear, dramatic
character of God's relation to the world in a way that must not
be lost.

What is needed is a concept of linear, dramatic existence
that takes more seriously the interaction between God and the
world. Then novelty need not be sheerly arbitrary, but can be
judged in terms of its enrichment of and contrast with what
has prepared the way for it. Then God is not the untouched
determiner of the end, but, as Herbert Butterfield pictures
him, much more like a composer who is writing the score a
few bars ahead of the orchestra, and taking account of their
harmonies and disharmonies as he proposes to them the new
score.[10] On such a view there can be no one fixed end determined in advance, but there can be a dependability in what

God intends, which brings together insights of Biblical and process perspectives.

One side of the new imagination calls for making God's functioning in relation to the world something that can be secularized and rationally examined; the other side is—perhaps surprisingly—that God is not the sole focus of wonder.

Reflective thinking has often sought for the focus of wonder in what is "ultimate," and this has often meant the most general properties of things. In process thinking, God is not ultimate in this sense. Whitehead speaks of creativity, the many, and the one as ultimates in his way of seeing things. But these exist only as embodied in God and the world. One may be amazed at creativity, but a concrete focus of wonder can be only where creativity is exemplified in an actual entity.

The real reshaping of traditional wonder comes when we see that God and the world are a basic pair of opposites that require each other. Each has to be secularized, but on the contrary each also has aspects which may, indeed must, be objects of wonder. Let us put it provocatively: the process God is not a jealous God who requires awe only of himself! In contrast to Bonhoeffer and Cox who build their theologies of secularization around the First Commandment: "Thou shalt have no other gods before me," we hold that the commandment itself needs to be rethought to see that both God and the world are foci of wonder. This shift is required if the "actual other" is to be a genuine center of wonder as we do experience the other, both the human person and the otherness of nature.

If we reshape our fundamental wonder to recognize that it is aroused by both God and the world, the question arises whether God remains the central focus of wonder. With striking clarity in the Biblical tradition, but also elsewhere, the struggle with God brought about the realization that God is the focus of both wonder and trust. The contemporary crisis of belief in God has more thoroughly criticized the sense of trust than the sense of wonder, so far as God is concerned. That is why the sense of wonder remains when no focus for it, no

God, can be discerned. God can be the central focus of wonder only if he is worthy of trust. It is my profound conviction that the widespread sense that there is no focus of trust springs in great measure from the fact that people are still testing their images of trust against the old God of infinite power. If we cannot be sure how things will come out, it is felt that we cannot trust. But if we move into the different perspective of the God who persuades rather than determines, and whose persuasion is admittedly limited by the massive inheritance from the past which sets the parameters of freedom, then we may judge differently about the many little indications, both in man and in nature, that existence is trustworthy. These indications may become signs pointing beyond themselves to a God whom we can trust, once we see that we do not have to look for the old kind of God who is totally in control.

For a vision of God and the world in which wonder and awe are not the prerogative of God alone, but in which God does remain the final focus of trust, we draw both on the insights of process thought and on the Biblical tradition. Both Whitehead and Hartshorne have shown how the God who requires to be secularized and is interactive with the world is also a God to be trusted because he is the source of trustworthy direction, the lure toward intensity and complexity of feeling. We join this insight with the Christian vision of God which, as we have seen, in its most distinct perspective recognizes God as involved in time and suffering, yet utterly trustworthy. The rich experience of moving through life in trust of such a God can be appropriated today in the midst of the decay of earlier certainties, if we are free from the rigidity of earlier Christian forms of understanding God.

Process Theology, Secularization, and Man

But it is not only in relation to God that process thinking can give a more adequate view of what is going on in secularization, and help us to see both the legitimacy and the limits of this process. For it is not only the trustworthiness of God that is in question, but the very coherence of man's selfhood. The two are closely related. Altizer astutely remarks that the death of God is a reflection of the dissolution of a uniquely modern form of consciousness.[11] The breakup of life into separate moments, and the quest for illumination in chance and inward "epiphanies" threaten to destroy loyalty and trust as much as does the eclipse of God. Most of the theology of secularization does not confront this problem, which is not adequately dealt with simply by turning man away from God to the world.

Here again we draw both on insights of process theology and on the Christian tradition. The process perspective has the immense advantage of showing how the self as a continuing series of occasions can be a real locus of freedom and sensitivity, reacting with the world and with other selves. This view makes the freedom and self-awareness of the self intelligible in a consistent way. But it does not necessarily emphasize responsibility, which implies the continuity of the self in time. The Biblical tradition of the struggle between man and God, taken with the process view, has a profundity that has not been exhausted despite the fragmentation of the modern imagination. True enough, the old-style concept of the almighty God did provoke a titanic exaggeration of selfhood in Western society, and if Altizer proclaims the death of this grotesque and exaggerated self, we can concur. But the alternative is not a dissection of the self into unrelated moments or a goal of ecstatic union that blurs all the centers of selfhood. Rather, we can move forward by coming to stand again in the perspective of the self in struggle with God which was hammered out in the fusion of common sense with the Biblical vision. It is the seriousness with which God takes the self that allows man to take himself seriously. This ancient insight can be recovered and trusted without escape to "another world," if these two resources are brought together. And this will open the way to a deepening of the life of the churches as communities of trust.

HOPE AND SECULARIZATION

Secularization, if it means focusing the attention of faith on the actual world of men and events, is an eminently hopeful trend. But as it is often presented, it is an unstable and transitional stance. Of course any position is transitional! We should not wish to develop a permanent point of no future movement. But the question is, In which direction shall we move as a result of the unfinished questions of the theology of secularization? The next move may well be to a sensitive but purely humanistic view of life. This is a more stable position than that of the theology of secularization, but it is not a position of hope. In today's world, a humanistic position can be held with Stoic resignation, but not with real openness to the future. If secularization as a movement toward human freedom and self-fulfillment is to move toward the future it glimpses, it will need a framework that can support its essentially Christian vision. The reshaping of the vision of both God and wonder which we propose can free man to be himself not in humanistic isolation from God and the world, but in interaction with God and the world.

V

Expecting the End

In the previous chapter we have shown that a process theology can provide a setting within which some of the central aspects of a Christian style of life, those comprehended under the term "secularization," can find a meaningful framework within which to grow: freedom, responsibility, and life in the world. The key image that put the movement from the static sacred to the social and historical world into relation with the Biblical and Christian tradition was the image of the struggle between man and God, for this image stresses both the seriousness with which concrete existence is taken by God, and his involvement in time.

Now we need to probe more closely into the process version of Christian hope by asking how we have to reinterpret the hope for a final end. Already the discussion of God as the "infinite" has made clear that a process perspective does not have any room for a literal final end. Yet in very early Christianity, at least, the expectation of the end was a powerful and central moment of faith. The question of how a modern theology relates to this early Christian hope is the more urgent because many sensitive spirits in our own time are once more using apocalyptic imagery—the symbolism of the coming end —to describe our situation. Is process thinking unaware of the

crisis symbolized by "the end," because it does not speak the
language of apocalypse? That is the question to which we
shall address ourselves in the present chapter.

When modern writers speak of ours as an apocalyptic time,
they mean that it is a time when the familiar framework
within which we live—the "house" of our spirit and imagination—is breaking up and threatening us with destruction. We
may speak in this way when we think of our social and historical existence. In this sphere the discovery and use of the
atomic bomb compelled many to look forward to an apocalyptic disaster for mankind, and such a New Testament passage
as II Peter 3:10 was widely used to describe the actual
historical fate that seemed to lie ahead of us: "Then the heav-
ens will pass away with a loud noise, and the elements will be
dissolved with fire, and the earth and the works that are upon
it will be burned up." Today, although this threat is still real
enough, the symbols of an all-encompassing disaster speak to
us most often in the words of those who are making us face
the ecological-population disaster which may make life on
earth impossible.

But in a wider sense, the language of apocalypse is appropriate because, regardless of our social and historical fate and
even if these concrete disasters do not fall upon us, we are losing the framework of inner meaning by which we locate ourselves and find our place in life. Expecting the end means
being shaken out of all our accepted certainties and being
forced to reexamine all the presuppositions by which we guide
our lives. As Amos N. Wilder puts it: "In this situation of disorientation, vertigo, and weightlessness, there are not only no
answers; there are no categories, no questions." He cites the
second chapter of Daniel as a parallel in ancient apocalyptic,
where Nebuchadnezzar not only cannot understand his dream,
but he has forgotten the dream itself.[1] In a way, that is where
we all are; we have forgotten the dream, and we need not just
answers, but new categories and new questions.

We do not believe that a Christian thinker can separate

himself from the sense of loss of meaning which strikes us everywhere in the writing and art of today. His quest for meaning is one that he shares with his world. He stands on the boundary between meaning and loss of meaning, and he does not affirm what he believes from some position of safety or immunity from threat, but he offers what he finds in his tradition and in his exploration both out of and into the dislocation which he lives in with his time. At the same time, both tradition and exploration can give leverage at just such a time as ours. In grappling with a new meaning for infinity as a religious symbol, we have already looked into our modern disorientation and lack of framework. There we saw that this very experience may itself provide an opening toward an essentially archaic sense of mystery before the loss of definite experience in the very repetition of infinite detail. But the more forward-looking response is a reforming of our imagination, by which we will not expect so much of "infinity." In the same way, here, we propose that insofar as "end" is a symbol of a complete answer to man's problems, we need to reform our imagination.

To propose this means that we are bold enough to believe that we can step out of the experience of disorientation which we find in the sense of impending doom, and ask whether there is not some other setting in which we can view it. We venture to do this as an act of Christian thinking fundamentally because the original Christian stance of expecting the end was a hopeful one. Despite all the symbolism of destruction that has been taken up into our modern imagination from traditional apocalyptic, this ancient Jewish and Christian form of faith was full of hope. Beyond the destruction it saw a new creation. To ask how far a new creation is implied or hoped for in the various modern forms of apocalyptic imagination is an important task, and one which has not been very much explored, but we cannot follow it further here. In Altizer's form of modern apocalyptic we found a powerful vision of new creation, but his insistence on total reversal and coincidence of opposites prevents him from talking about the new creation except in the symbols of death and descent into hell. Something like this would be true of many others who, in different and often less religious language, are trying to express a modern vision of apocalypse. To many of them it will appear perverse if this discussion of the end bypasses most of the symbols of destruction and struggles directly with the symbols of hope. That may seem to be a way of escaping the real problems. It is intended, however, as a way of getting a new slant on the very problems which appear directly to the imagination in the symbols of destruction. The stance of faith as immersion in the suffering and death of the world is the only side of faith which many modern Christians can express. They have exposed the shallowness of a comfortable faith which rests in the confidence that it is somehow exempt from the agony of other men. Nevertheless, we believe that the apocalyptic pattern, even though we have to reinterpret it drastically, can point us toward the kind of structure in which hope can thrive. In any case, if a modern vision is to translate the early Christian apocalyptic faith, it must finally be a vision of hope and not of destruction.

What follows may perhaps be even more taxing on the reader, because it will be far more historical in detail than any earlier part of this book. It is a structural analysis of early Christian hope, and the Jewish hope that gave it its language, in order to see what elements in it can be coherent with and can extend the process structure that we have sketched out above.

End as Total Loss of Differentiation or End as the End of a Stage

Hope in apocalyptic eschatology, both Jewish and Christian, may be most simply put as "expectation of the end." What it is to live confronting the expected end is what we are trying to understand and to bring over into our modern situation in which the end seems to have nothing to do with God. We begin by noticing that the stance of confronting the end is not so simple as it appears to be. "Confronting the end" as a total end, the dissolution of all differentiated reality, is quite different from confronting a drastic transformation of existence within which a differentiated future nonetheless continues. The end may be approached as something total or as the end of a stage. Both approaches appear in the New Testament, or rather, elements pointing both ways can be found. Nowhere is there a full expression of hope as confronting a total end; the nearest approach is found in two striking passages from Paul, both in central eschatological affirmations:

Then comes the end, when he delivers the kingdom to God the Father. . . . That God may be all in all. (I Cor. 15:24, 28.)

For from him and through him and to him are all things. (Rom. 11:36.)

Each of these passages uses a symbolism in which all differentiated aspects of reality "end" in God; they approach the symbolism of a total end. As such, this language indicates the affinity of apocalyptic thought and gnosticism, in which the longing for totality, for total presence, is even more pronounced. It is, of course, quite true that in their respective contexts neither of these passages should be pressed so far. Thus W. G. Kümmel rightly remarks about I Cor. 15:28 that Paul did not envisage a loss of differentiation among God, Christ, and the believers.[2] Nonetheless, it is not accidental that the passages are there, for they indicate the thrust toward totality that is a characteristic of apocalyptic and show that the end can function as a symbol for the summing up and inclusion of everything in the divine reality. This thrust toward total presence with loss of differentiation is much more marked in gnosticism (in part a descendant from apocalyptic eschatology), which developed an elaborate mythology of the stages leading to the reabsorption of reality in God.

The thrust toward totality finds natural expression in the use of symbols of the beginning to express the end. It has long been remarked that a prime characteristic of apocalyptic imagery is the principle that the end-time is like the time of beginning (Gunkel). "From him, and through him, and to him are all things." Of many examples from earlier apocalyptic we cite one: in the Apocalypse of Weeks in Enoch 93, 91, history is divided into ten weeks; God rules the first and then again the tenth week. One meaning of this hope of a return to the beginning was the hope for a return to the undifferentiated point of origin.

Most New Testament symbolism, and most apocalyptic symbolism generally, does not point toward a "total end." It is interesting to note that the popular and total-sounding modern term "the *eschaton*" is unknown in eschatological literature, as far as I can discover.[3] A group of things must happen at the end, not just a single thing, and their outcome is not commonly expected to be a total loss of differentiation. As far as the expected group of events is concerned, the details are most varied, and this variety can in good part be attributed to the fact that apocalyptic books grew by the accretion of various traditions. But the fact that a complex series of events was expected, and—more importantly—the fact that what followed the end was typically conceived statically but nonetheless in differentiated fashion, testify to the importance with which it was believed God regarded concrete human existence. Concrete human existence included, with varying emphasis, both a concrete people and concrete individuals. Part of the reason for the variety in the symbolization of the last things was the mixture of these two concerns. On the one hand, the "people" must come to be what God intends a people to be, and on the other, each self—commonly each self within a particular group—is taken seriously by God and will be taken up into the fulfillment and not simply allowed to pass into nonexistence. Thus the "end" is typically conceived as the end of a stage, even though the succeeding stage is not imagined as including further history or development. One factor that held in check the thrust toward a total end—a total loss of differentiation—was the conviction that God took differentiated, concrete existence so seriously that he would, in one way or another, take it up into the final fulfillment.

At the same time, it was believed that only by passing through what was in some sense the end of existence as now known could the people, collectively or individually, come to be what God intended. Thus the end, both in the New Testament and in apocalyptic eschatology generally, can be characterized as "reversal," for this whole literature springs from an experience of alienation, and it finds a continuation of present existence unthinkable. The outcome is, therefore, thought of as a reversal of the present. The emphasis may lie on the reversal of the inner disposition: sin and the aggressive drives that produce conflict will be done away. Or the emphasis may lie on the change in outward circumstances: the enemy or the demonic powers he expresses will be done away. The change will bring about a reversal in the status of believers over against the worldly powers—"The first shall be last and last first." Thus "world" bears a negative value in eschatological literature; it is understood to be a power that opposes life. The negative attitude toward the world and the expectation of reversal may be expressed in asceticism. However, physical things are not usually felt to be bad in themselves, but only as they stand in the way of community—an ancient motif in Israelite religion, sometimes expressed, as at Qumran, in a preference for an antiurban sociological structure. In the New Testament the obstacles to community are more typically sensed as internal to the self, and thus interfering with social relations, so that the world is something internal as well as something external. We cannot follow this difficult problem of the meanings of the world further here. The expectation of the end as reversal arises when existence is felt as disoriented, alienated, perhaps hardly bearable.

Yet one must ask, Does this kind of faith really expect total reversal? Later, more consistently dualistic thinkers, the Gnostics, posited a divine spark in the potential Gnostic, which might be obscured or forgotten, but which was nonetheless there; the reversal of everything else meant the coming to light of this hidden reality. Similarly, in apocalyptic thought, there is already something good present, however threatened it may be. Most often, as in Daniel, Qumran, and the New Testament, there is a tiny good community which already expresses something of God's intention, even though in thwarted fashion. The community has something given to it to which it can hold fast—in Jewish apocalyptic most prominently the Torah. In the New Testament the whole balance of the apocalyptic contrast between the evil present and the good future is upset by the faith that something new has already come into being. The reality of Jesus Christ is so powerful and transforming that it can only be described in symbols derived from hope, "end" symbols such as Christ, resurrection, and Kingdom of God, even though the transformation of reality experienced in faith does not transform the external social structure nor completely transform the self.[4] Thus the concept of reversal needs to be handled with some care. There is a tendency for the hope for reversal to be expressed in antitheses which sound total, but when one inspects these closely, one finds that the enthusiasm for reversal springs precisely from the present reality of something that is the basis for hope.

Hope for the end as reversal of the evil world leads naturally to the question of hope and history. Before turning to this, however, we should note an aspect of eschatological hope that has not yet been singled out: the end is coming soon. This is so obvious to the apocalyptic believer that he seldom analyzes why it must be so. Indeed, it has often been observed that the more improbable the hope of redemption becomes "empirically," the more passionate becomes the eschatological faith that the end is coming soon.[5] "He is at the very doors." Whatever the connections are between Old Testament prophecy and apocalyptic, this point is clearly held in common. The "soon" is an index of the intensity of faith.[6] This is the sort of faith which has called forth the question of some modern analysts of the truth value of religious statements: How much contrary evidence would it require to disprove your faith? The apocalyptist, although not grasping the problem in the same reflective way, responds in an opposite fashion. The stronger the conflict between the heart of his existence and what he finds to be negative factors, the more strongly he affirms that the end is at hand. This statement needs to be modified to this extent, that thinking about the end also involved a kind of speculative distancing from the situation of crisis, and a study of various ways of calculating the end. Within this perspective, it appears that one of the earliest apocalyptists, Daniel, was the most explicit about the exact time of the end, while repeated disappointment of calculation led later writers to be more circumspect.[7] It should also be said that the awareness of the imminence of the end involved a tension between faith in God's freedom to determine the end as he chose, on the one hand, and reflection about the question whether men could do anything to hasten the end, on the other.[8] As noted above, the sense of time moving quickly to its end is a way of grasping the reality of what is in the process of being given in faith. Living in a fragmented reality, the apocalyptist does not venture to seek any kind of present coherence but affirms that that to which he is committed will come to be the prevalent reality.

APOCALYPTIC AND HISTORY

We come to the question of apocalyptic and history. This has been much discussed, and we can only touch on it here. The apocalyptic resolution is relevant, as noted above, both to the individual and to the group. As far as the individual is concerned, there is to be a sorting out of the good from the bad, which (usually) will be followed by an everlasting life for both. The fundamental driving force behind this faith was the need to affirm God's justice, without denying that elements of desire for reward and for revenge were also present. A faith in future rewards and punishments does not necessarily have anything to do with history as such. In the New Testament, however, and usually in apocalyptic eschatology, faith in future rewards and punishments is joined with a concern for history, and becomes an expression of faith in the outcome of history as well as of individual existence. The two belong together because the existence of the self is so closely bound up with its social group and history. The typical apocalyptic view of history regards both the past and the future as better than the present. This is easy to understand as coming from situations of crisis. It is important to see that the various speculative schemes of history that apocalyptic developed have as one important function the safeguarding of the past from which the community received its faith—that past was not as alienated from God as is the present. At the same time, this essentially conservative view of the past was combined with a sense that things are tending somewhere, that faith has been given a clue to what they are tending toward. In the New Testament this side is much more significant than the schematizing of the past, which receives little attention, although the fact that Christ soon became a figure of the past resulted in the reappearance of the conservative motif.

In comparison with the prophetic comments on history, apocalyptic tends toward the elaboration of a deterministic scheme, and at the same time tends toward an interest in all history.[9] The determinism is related to the unfavorable situation of the believer; he cannot think that he can get himself out of the situation he is in, and must believe that God will do this for him. Determinism, as in Calvinism, is an expression of wonder at the glory of God. It is also connected, however, with the attitude of speculative distancing that tries not only to find God's will for a present crisis but also to see an overall meaning for the whole course of human existence. Thus the determinism of apocalyptic is related to its universalism. It is true that the "universal history" of apocalyptic is seldom or never fully universal—the historical schemes often do not begin with the Creation, for instance, but at some recent point such as the Flood or the exile. However, these schemes do reveal an interest in the broad question of how all history fits together. Insofar as they are successful, such schemes make use of an element that we may call the concept of "waste." A large part of history is, from the point of view of the final outcome, waste. In this way the more individualistic concept of rewards and punishments after death was linked to the concept of historical process culminating in the creation of a true community, a "holy city." The apocalyptist accepts the waste of history, sometimes without any pangs, but also, in the most sensitive expressions, with a real sense of the tragic pressure which this way of thinking creates. Paul and IV Ezra both struggle with the waste of history, IV Ezra in the mood of wondering whether history is worthwhile at all for its meager results of a few righteous people, Paul with the aim of affirming that in spite of the seeming erratic course of history and its waste, "all," that is, Jews and Gentiles, will be saved in the end.[10]

Though the New Testament writers share many typical concerns of apocalyptic writers generally, the New Testament books shaped by this perspective have their own characteristic difference in that the present is not an empty time, but is filled with a new reality that is described in the ultimate symbols of the end. This is not a complete distinction from other apocalyptic, since all apocalyptic has some present reality to which it clings. Nonetheless, this feature is a strong mark of the use made of apocalyptic symbolism in the New Testament, a use that produces a tension between present and future as foci of faith which is not usual in apocalyptic. Most apocalyptic focuses much more strongly on the future and finds the present empty. In the New Testament, the present already has, for faith, the fundamental character that it is hoped will completely characterize the future.

In this connection we may note a final characteristic of apocalyptic expectation of the end: although its stance is often one of passivity, this kind of faith may enlist the believer in work which is part of what God is doing to bring about the end. This is a prominent feature of New Testament eschatology, most obviously in Paul, with his high sense of vocation to take part in the work of God, but it is present in the Synoptic Gospels as well. Volz remarks the contrast between the passivity of much apocalyptic and the confidence and energy for work which the New Testament shows.[11] He did not see, as we can see after the publication of the materials from Qumran, that energetic participation in the eschatological process might also be a mark of nationalistic eschatology.

Thus we see in the expectation of the end a complex of elements. Although there is a thrust toward grasping the end as a total loss of differentiation, this is not the prevailing image, which is rather that of the end as a series of stages that will lead to a static, yet still differentiated, mode of existence. Among other things, the images of continuing differentiated existence express the seriousness with which, it is believed, God is concerned for concrete human existence. The meaning of the end is strongly felt as a reversal of the present, but a close study shows that the hope for reversal can be held because something which cannot be abandoned is felt to be already real. The intensity of the faith is expressed in the temporal form that the end will be soon. As part of a move to stand back and survey the whole of reality and fit it all into the perspective of faith, the history of the community serves as the starting point for a grasp of all history as intended to culminate in the great "end," although this view can be achieved only by regarding most of history as waste, a loss that was severely felt by some who lived in this perspective. In the New Testament, a different shape is given to the usual form of apocalyptic expectation by the conviction that a new and final reality is already present or in process of becoming present. While in other, particularly nationalistic, forms of apocalyptic,

believers may be enlisted to take part in the process leading
toward the end, this conviction is a particular characteristic of
New Testament eschatology.

HOPE FOR THE END AND CHRISTIAN EXISTENCE

All this is mythical thinking, and as Northrop Frye says,
myth is imagination at or near the limits of desire.[12] The
imaginative fancy is obvious enough in apocalyptic, both Jewish and Christian, although it is worth noticing that both the
Synoptics and Paul are restrained at this point. Nonetheless, it
is easy to dismiss the whole structure as wish projection. Although recognizing this side of the apocalyptic imagination,
we hold that any viable human perspective must express itself
in "mythical" ways and that any view of life which takes the
future seriously must make a place for the element of wish. Although theology has to clarify the mythical and symbolic
affirmations, it cannot eliminate them without eliminating the
perspective itself.

Of the many ways of clarifying the meaning of Christian
faith, we choose to begin with Christian existence. To set forth
the structure of Christian existence is a major task in itself, but
it can briefly be said here that Christian existence is characterized by love as a self-transcendence which puts the self at the
disposal of the other.[13] Christian existence is never fully realized, and to the extent that it is realized, the self-transcendence which it expresses is enabled by a sense of receiving life and the coming moment as a gift; we love because
we are loved. While always mediated through some concrete
encounter, the sense of gift has been seen as ultimately God's
gift, and the figure of Jesus Christ has been both paradigm
and in some sense channel of the acceptance by which one is
given the freedom of love. Apocalyptic eschatology was a
principal symbolic tool for the grasp of reality both for Jesus
and for most of his first interpreters. But the modern thinker is
not concerned with apocalyptic merely because of its external

association with the paradigmatic figure of his faith. More profoundly, apocalyptic eschatology brings to expression elements that have always been seen as central to the structure of Christian existence itself. The erosion of traditional forms of faith has led many modern men to write of love without putting the traditional stress on hope, but the structure of Christian existence in love is most precarious unless it is able to affirm hope. For one thing, love is not just a concern for another in the moment of encounter (as is often eloquently said today); it is also a concern for the other's future. Love is a "walking along the way with him." Thus, although in its more intense form, Christian existence means a disregard for one's future, this is correlated with a concern with another's future, which brings both immediate practical hopes and long-range hopes into relevance. Furthermore, despite the fragmentariness of life, the basis of Christian existence—the sense of receiving life and the next moment as a gift—implies that the future is ultimately trustworthy, or, in traditional language, that the future is in God's hands.

Despite the frequent renunciation of the future by many contemporary theologians, the structure of Christian existence itself thus points to and assumes a future. Fully to interpret the structure of hope that arises from the nature of Christian existence would involve interpreting the central focus of New Testament faith—Jesus Christ—from a process perspective, especially since the eschatological points of view themselves were reshaped by the awareness of the new in Jesus. For if we take as the clue to the distinction between hope and dream that hope already participates in the reality for which it hopes,[14] a fully adequate exposition of hope in the New Testament will have to deal with the reality which the believer encounters and identifies as Jesus Christ.

The final chapter of this book will present an interpretation of Christ as the center of the future as hope. At this point we shall move instead directly from the implications of the structure of Christian existence itself to a process interpretation of it.

Eschatological Hope in Process Perspective

From a process point of view, the whole image of final end has to be regarded as an image to be interpreted, for it is central to process thinking that creativity never comes to an end. The image of a static perfection—so frequent in apocalyptic symbolism—is not an appropriate symbol of the ultimate future in process categories. Total loss of differentiation is even more alien to a process perspective. Indeed, the introduction of a new conceptualization of infinity or totality—a "serially enriched totality"—is one of the most important theological contributions of process philosophy, for this is an important alternative to a nondifferentiated totality which is the other principal way of ultimately interpreting the "final end." A process view of the future has two ways of interpreting the symbol of the final end. One line of interpretation, drawing on the thought of Teilhard de Chardin, would affirm that though the general structure of process thought is open to an indefinite number of cosmic epochs or particular ways in which reality is structured, in point of fact we find two—the epoch in which we find ourselves, and another which is partly becoming real and which will assimilate and preserve the higher reality of this epoch.[15] This is a fruitful line to explore, but it will not be followed here. Remaining with the open-ended character of process thought, "end" will here be regarded as a mythological symbol, embodying two meanings that can be explicated in a framework of process thought: the meaning of ultimacy and the meaning of fulfillment or functional participation in a later reality.

The forward reach of Christian existence may unreflectively understand itself as moving toward a final end but reflective clarification of the symbol will point to these interpretations of end. The former meaning—the meaning of ultimacy—is the aspect of confronting the end that is emphasized by the existentialist interpretation of eschatology. In Christian existence, the ultimacy of the moment of decision, its unique irreversibility, is suggested by the symbol of each moment's having to bear the weight of that definitive significance which the end has. Rudolf Bultmann concludes his book on history with the well-known lines, "Do not look around yourself into universal history, you must look into your own personal history. . . . In every moment slumbers the possibility of being the eschatological moment. You must awaken it." [16] Along with existentialist thinking, process thought, with its stress on actual occasions as "the final real things of which the world is made up," [17] must understand existence confronting the end as meaning that each actual occasion has, or has the possibility of being of, ultimate significance, and of being an "eschatological moment." But unlike existentialist theology, process thought can join this emphasis with an insight into how the moment reaches beyond itself.

Thus process thinking opens the way to doing more with the second meaning of "end," the end as that to which one looks forward as a fulfillment of the process in which one is involved, or as the functional participation of the passing moments in a later reality. Christian existence, and that for which Christian existence cares, are, despite the brokenness and loss that are so evident, known to be taken up into the future. A process view takes freedom to be one of the constituent aspects of how reality works, and therefore no specific shape of the future can be determined in advance. On the other hand, however, the process view that each occasion is given its potentialities not only by the subjective aim established for it by God but also by the actual data which its past offers it, provides a most meaningful framework within which to interpret this meaning of the symbol "end." Though renouncing the aim of disclosing in advance what the shape of the future will be, the process view holds that the bold hope of Christian existence is justified, that the future will embody the creative gifts to it of each successive act. That the particular utilization of these gifts may not be what the giver anticipates means that a process interpretation of hope, like apocalyptic eschatology, has to include a concept of waste. But the other side of this situation is that the resources which the present contributes to the future may be used in unexpectedly creative ways. These reflections are particularly relevant to the interpretation of the motif of fulfillment in its aspect of participation in the eschatological process, an aspect of hope that is strong in early Christianity, in which the believer finds that he is called to take part in the work of God. To this we shall devote the next chapter.

The baffling problem of evil is not "solved" in this perspective, but important new light is cast upon it when we conceive of God not as in absolute control, but rather as a powerful lure to the good, who cannot prevent, but shares in suffering.[18]

A related question is whether a process view does not threaten the coherence of Christian existence itself, which may be so modified in the course of time that it loses its distinctiveness. A process perspective can offer no guarantee that this will not take place. But neither does it have to be interpreted in such a way that all historical distinctiveness becomes fluid. As a philosophical position, process philosophy does not accord priority to any particular structure that expresses intensity. But the theologian who is using process categories can affirm that within the conditions of human existence, a particular form of existence—Christian existence—is not only unique but also in its own line of development is unsurpassable.[19] Such a theology can be fully open to new forms of expression of Christian existence and to participation in dialogue with other positions, which will uncover new aspects of its relation to these other views. Thus a process theology need not threaten the coherence or distinctiveness of Christian existence, the actual continuation of which will depend, among other things, on its own inner unity and its communicability.

So far hope has been discussed only in terms of continuing series of actual occasions. This is the proper place to begin, since a process view of hope, directing it in the first place to the actual occasions in which hope acts, has in common with Moltmann's interpretation and with the existentialist interpretation of eschatology a strong thrust toward action in the present as the concomitant of hope, and grounds its hope on the openness of the future and on the confidence that God will be active in the future as in the present. But process thinking also attempts to clarify faith's view of God himself, in contrast to some theologies which regard this as an illegitimate undertaking. So far as hope is concerned, the possibility of novelty is grounded in the boundless potentiality of the primordial nature of God. But concrete hope is more directly related to the function of the consequent nature of God. In his consequent nature, God constantly receives each occasion as it occurs at its proper rank and retains it everlastingly. Over against the loss and "waste" in the process of actual occasions, here there is a preservation of what is worth preserving, although there is waste in that the trivial is relegated to triviality, and what is important to us may be judged trivial. It is the confidence that in spite of the waste in the world, the occasions that pass are not finally lost, but recognized everlastingly in God, that gives an ultimate ground to hope in a process perspective.

Such a view recognizes the element of God's taking each concrete occasion of existence seriously, a characteristic that we noted as an aspect of apocalyptic eschatology. Within a process perspective, the usual way of explicating this aspect of hope—the hope that that which is of worth will not be lost—is through the preservation of worth in the memory of God, in the consequent nature of God.[20] This insight is fundamental for a process theology of Christian existence.

Before we try to assess the adequacy of this kind of interpretation of the end for our own situation, and in confronting the crisis of meaning mentioned at the beginning of this chapter, it is important to look more concretely at hope in the New Testament, to see how the broad categories worked out here were filled in with specific content. To that task we now turn.

VI
Participating in the Future

ACTIVE AND PASSIVE HOPE

The previous chapter analyzed the way in which men await the end in apocalyptic faith, and showed how this faith can be understood in a process perspective. Apocalyptic thought, however, is itself extremely varied. Particularly important is the tension in it suggested by the word "await" in the phrase "awaiting the end." For this word has a very passive sound which is actually quite appropriate to much apocalyptic. If the world is felt to be so bad that only God can change it, then it is natural for the man of faith to fall into a passive stance. Often the apocalyptic books speak a strongly deterministic language, most vividly on the point that the end is coming at a time fixed in advance by God. This determinism expresses both wonder and hope; God will mysteriously bring something good out of the present evil situation.

But even the most deterministic faith is also faith; it has a place for the human response of trust. And some forms of apocalyptic are extremely activist and even revolutionary. The faith of the New Testament is for the most part a faith of active hope, in which the believer is enlisted to participate in the movement toward what he hopes for. This chapter will look particularly at this motif of participation in hope. It is important to make this emphasis clear, because both ordinary believers and scholars have often overlooked the response of participation, and have thought of the hope for the end purely in terms of what God would do.

It would be natural to ask about the hope of Jesus himself, but to try to work through the complicated question of just what we can know about Jesus would take us far beyond the scope of this chapter. Instead, we shall focus on the particular kinds of apocalyptic hope that are expressed in the first three Gospels, the Synoptic Gospels. For these Gospels express one of the central forms of early Christianity, and they have repeatedly been an avenue to the rediscovery of some of the impact of early Christianity. The profile of hope that we find in them will be extremely important for testing the compatibility of process categories with early Christian hope.

Within the Synoptic Gospels, we choose two kinds of tradition: Mark and the "sayings tradition" embodied in Matthew and Luke. Mark, the second Gospel, was written toward the end of the first Christian generation, and it was apparently the first "Gospel," the first book of this form, to be written. Some of the sayings of Jesus appear in Mark, but by and large the "sayings tradition" represents another form of early Christian message, a form that we now find in the largely parallel sayings of Jesus found in Matthew and Luke. These sayings, now found in the Sermon on the Mount, for instance, existed as a separate collection of sayings of Jesus before they came into Matthew and Luke. Though there are great difficulties in establishing the exact contents of this collection of sayings, we can be confident that we understand its main thrust.[1] It communicated the meaning of Jesus not by emphasizing his death, but by reporting what were remembered as his most important sayings. We shall call this collection of sayings by its traditional scholarly name "Q," and we shall not be asking how accurately it or Mark represents Jesus' actual words, but simply what style of faith and hope these two sources, Mark and Q, present.

HOPE IN Q

Q was a collection of sayings of the Lord, but it was not teaching as that term is used to contrast with preaching. Q was, on the contrary, a style of proclamation, and it is one of the oddities of New Testament scholarship that it was so long fashionable to regard it as a collection of "teachings" which were a supplement, coming after the presentation of Christian preaching, to show men how, once they had responded to the preaching, they were to behave in daily life.[2] Such a systematic separation of teaching and preaching did take place in a later stage of the life of the church, but not in that early stage during which Q was gathered together. The only reason why the "teaching" theory of Q was so long-lived was the presupposition that there was only one form of early Christian proclamation, the proclamation centering on the death of Jesus that appears in different versions in Paul and Mark. Once we set aside this presupposition and listen to what the sayings of Q have to say, it will be very clear that they carry a strong note of proclamation, that they are in fact a different form of early Christian preaching.

Q centers on the word of the Jesus who is known as the resurrected, exalted Lord, and for the historian of Jesus one of the central problems is to disengage the remembered words of Jesus from the words heard as words of the exalted Lord. But we shall not be concerned to analyze Q from this point of view—even though it is clear that this collection of sayings represents a process, a process moving from an early Palestinian community into a Greek-speaking community that had put their impress upon Q before the sayings came into the hands of Matthew and Luke. Rather, we shall try to look at the shape of hope in Q itself, leaving open the question of the historical Jesus.

H. E. Tödt has proposed that Q is to be understood as arising in a community which found their bond with Jesus renewed by the resurrection, and carried his proclamation forward into their own time and situation—without, however, giving particular attention to the meaning of Jesus' death for faith.[3] Though in fact the community mingled remembered words of Jesus and prophetically given words of the resurrected Lord, they did not fuse the figures of the earthly Jesus and the coming Son of Man, instead keeping a clear distinction between the earthly life of Jesus as a time of conflict and rejection, and the future total triumph of the Son of Man.[4] With this position I am in basic agreement, though not with the details of Tödt's analysis of the Son of Man sayings.

It is obvious that the sayings of Q present a most vigorous hope—whatever we are to make of it—a hope cast in the eschatological form of the impending coming of the Son of Man and of the Kingdom of God, for both these terms are central in Q. On the one hand, the hope of Q has a strongly dialectical character. The empty present is contrasted with the filled future, as in the Lucan form of the Beatitudes, which are probably earlier in form than Matthew's. On the other hand, Q contains a strong element of realized eschatology, that is, faith that the present already has the character of the end, as in the saying, "But if it is by the finger of God that I cast out demons, then the kingdom of God has come upon you" (Luke 11:20). Here hope is the expansion and fulfillment of something already present. Let us look at this pattern of expectation more closely.

First, we note that though the death of Jesus is not a motif of Q—much to the sorrow of those who want to impose a uniformity on early Christianity—the motif of "death through life" *is* prominent and recurring in the collection.

Whoever does not bear his own cross and come after me, cannot be my disciple. (Luke 14:27.)

He who finds his life will lose it, and he who loses his life for my sake will find it. (Matt. 10:39.)

Blessed are you when men hate you, and when they exclude you and revile you. . . . Behold, your reward is
great in heaven. (Luke 6:22-23.)

This motif of "finding through losing" is not simply presented as a command to the believer; it is presented also as
Jesus' way, though through his life rather than his death:

Foxes have holes, and birds of the air have nests; but
the Son of man has nowhere to lay his head. (Matt. 8:20.)

A disciple is not above his teacher. (Matt. 10:24.)

Thus insofar as hope is understood as pointing toward the
fulfillment of ordinary human goal-directed strivings, the first
impact of the message of Q is the negative one: it is only
through death that there is life, and only in giving up is there
finding. At this point the message of Q is at one with the
"death of Christ" centered proclamation of Mark and Paul.

If we look beyond this initial negative note, we find three
motifs in the sayings material that engage our attention. First
there is the already mentioned motif of realized eschatology.
It is a striking fact that Dodd, who developed the view that
Jesus' message was one of realized eschatology, found most of
the sayings that express a newly present eschatological reality
in Q.[5]

But if it is by the finger of God that I cast out demons,
then the kingdom of God has come upon you. (Luke
11:20.)

Woe to you Chorazin! woe to you, Bethsaida! for if the
mighty works done in you had been done in Tyre and
Sidon, they would have repented long ago in sackcloth
and ashes. (Matt. 11:21.)

Something greater than Jonah is here. . . . Something
greater than Solomon is here. (Matt. 12:41-42.)

As we read them in their setting in Q, those sayings convey
an immense sense of the new presence of divine reality, which

carries with it a likewise powerful sense that this divine reality is moving forward to its fulfillment. Students who concentrate on the Christological passages in Q may miss the point that this present eschatology is the key to the inclusion in Q of so much of the wisdom-type material about the conduct of the present life. Wisdom was concerned with the understanding and management of life, with the short-time span of human self-consciousness. What happens in Q is that the lore of this tradition is transposed into the radical key of *agapē:* this is the new presence of the divine. Openness to the other's future through the route of loss of concern for one's own—that is what gives concreteness to the "life through death" motif of Q that we have sketched. Perhaps we do not need to illustrate this further than to refer to the Golden Rule, a prudential saying about how to smooth the rough edges of life in one's own interest, which, transposed into the setting of Q, conveys the claim of the other, as does the claim, more radical in itself, of love for the enemy.[6] The shift of hope from one's own self-projection to concern for the other brings to light the more profound question of hope, not only for the Christian tradition but for human seeking generally: the vision of God's concern for the other leads to hope for *his* future.

This concern leads naturally to the second motif in the understanding of the present time which is prominent in the sayings source: the emphasis on the community. The community shares the rejection and at the same time the authority of its Lord. It is the present eschatological reality—the rejection of Jesus in the past can be forgiven, but the rejection of the spirit at work in the community cannot be forgiven.[7] Here, at quite an early stage in the history of Christianity, we can see the problem of Catholicism: the problem of how the continuing presence of a community of grace can be assured.

The forward-looking elements in this community's life constitute the third motif which calls for attention. They can be classified under the headings of *reward* and *participation.* The reward motif is prominent, as it is in every type of Synoptic tradition. The Beatitudes are cast in this form. More explicit is the saying about treasure on earth and treasure in heaven (or with God) (Matt. 6:19-21). The close relation of the reward motif to the figure of Christ is shown in the saying, fundamental for Q, as Tödt has pointed out: "Every one who acknowledges me before men, the Son of man also will acknowledge before the angels of God" (Luke 12:8).[8] We shall not follow this motif of reward farther here, except to say that it clearly reveals the understanding that beyond the death of self the believer participates in a reality which is taken up and fulfilled in the final consummation.

The element of fulfillment is even clearer in the other forward-looking element: the motif of participation. God is doing a work. It is God's work, and men cannot force it, but the community is called into the same task as its Lord: "The harvest is plentiful, but the laborers are few; pray therefore the Lord of the harvest to send out laborers into his harvest" (Luke 10:2). "I *send* you" uses the word "send forth," with its strong connotation of participation (Luke 10:3). "He who hears you hears me" (Luke 10:16). Though it is more characteristic of the Marcan tradition, Q also has the term "follow," which does not mean a passive coming after someone, but expresses participation in the Master's task (Matt. 10:38). The forward direction of this participation is most strongly expressed in the faith that the community would also take part in the future work of the Son of Man: You "will also sit on twelve thrones, judging the twelve tribes of Israel" (Matt. 19:28; cf. I Cor. 6:3). This conviction of being called to participate in the eschatological process, which appears clearly in Q, reaches its height in the New Testament, of course, in Paul with his tremendous sense of apostolic vocation.[9] It is not so sharply expressed in Q, no doubt partly because Q expresses the sense of vocation of a community, while in Paul we have a highly individualized self-consciousness. Though the material in Q offers little reflection on this subject, the reward motif and the participation motif reinforce each other in expressing a stance in which it is self-evident that beyond the negation of self there lies a new life in which one already participates, and in which one's goal-directed strivings are not just self-projection, but are part of the process of God's work, and hence take on real significance for the future, being taken up into the eschatological consummation. At the same time, we should not fail to note that these motifs of reward and of fulfillment are matched by an extensive group of sayings about the need to "watch" (Luke 12:39-46; cf. 17:26-27, 35) which emphasize the fact that the believing community does not have a secure present possession of the power which is at work in it.

If this analysis of hope in Q will stand up, it reminds us of what a remarkable pattern of early Christian proclamation this was: one that strongly emphasized the death and new life of the believer, but did so by paralleling this with the humiliation in life of Jesus, followed by his resurrection, rather than emphasizing his death; one that powerfully expressed a realized eschatology and a sense of the unique role of the chosen community—motifs that reappear later both in gnosticism and in Catholicism—and one that still maintained as well a strong sense of the incompleteness and hope orientation of the life of the believer. We shall in our conclusion try to look at some of the questions which this faith poses for our interpretation of it. Here we can raise only one further question about Q: What if the historical analysis on which this presentation is based is faulty, and there never was such a collection of tradition as we have assumed? In a way that would be embarrassing, and some of the points made above would be rather shaky, to say the least. But basically the point is that these motifs do occur in very early Christianity. If the historical criticism that uncovers Q is faulty, then these motifs become somewhat subsidiary to a more monolithic mainstream of tradition. But they are still there, and at bottom the interpreter of the significance of early Christianity has to deal with much the same range of problems. Before we look further at what these are, we should compare our findings from Q with what appears in the Gospel of Mark.

HOPE IN MARK

If we turn to Mark, we find many of the same themes. There is the characteristic difference that Mark is a story; it cannot be transposed into a nonhistorical word as the materials in Q can be. The story focuses emphatically on the element in early Christian tradition that is surprisingly unemphasized in Q: the death of Christ. Correspondingly, the emphasis on newly achieved divine reality—what Dodd called realized eschatology—which is prominent in Q, is present in Mark in more veiled fashion: the "secret" of who Jesus is.[10] In Mark, in other words, the tension of "life through death" is presented more intensely or inexorably: one can scarcely ever, in Mark, look for more than a moment at the side of life and joy without being reminded that it comes only through death and suffering. As in Q, the first word of Mark to the human future of self-projection is a negative one. This is the point of the saying about the receptivity of children. They do not have to project themselves. They can accept. (Mark 10:15.)

Though it is subsidiary to his purpose to present what we would call "unaided human effort," the futility of this, from Mark's point of view, is shown not only by the bungling of someone who tried to resist at Jesus' arrest, and of someone else who had to escape naked (Mark 14:47, 51-52), but also more importantly by the story of Peter's denial (Mark 14:66-72). To all this sort of effort, as well as to the religiously oriented striving of the rich young ruler (Mark 10:17-22), the word of Mark is a sharp "No."

Mark identifies the believing community with Christ, as Q does, in the sense that for the community as for Jesus during his lifetime, the deliverance from the situation of tension is still future. The believing community, coming after the resurrection, is not thereby exempted from the same trials that fell upon Jesus.

What Mark says about the disciples who were with Jesus

applies still to the community for which he was writing, and one important meaning of the projection of the fulfillment into the future is that "historical existence," as James M. Robinson calls it in his *The Problem of History in Mark*, an existence of struggle, continues for the church as for Jesus.[11] There is not so much concrete illustration of how this community is to exist in Mark as in Q, but the main lines are strikingly similar— drawing at times, of course, on the same "Jesus" tradition for material. For the inner relationships of the community, we have the striking saying: "Whoever would be great among you must be your servant, and whoever would be first among you must be slave of all" (Mark 10:43-44), where the future as the future of the other is opened by the closing off of one's own projection of himself into the future, just as in a group of Q passages discussed above.

It is not necessary to analyze the present under its negative aspect of persecution, which is so strongly asserted by Mark in ch. 13 and elsewhere. As in all eschatological thought, this present is given meaning by a future orientation, but the striking thing about Mark is how firm he is about not letting the believer off easily, not letting him escape into the "not yet." Thus: "If your foot causes you to sin, cut it off; it is better for you to enter life lame than with two feet to be thrown into hell" (Mark 9:45); here the future remains of unquestioned significance, but the thrust is all on the present. Something of the same thrust can be seen in the well-known passage on reward:

Peter began to say to him, "Lo, we have left everything and followed you." Jesus said, "Truly, I say to you, there is no one who has left house or brothers or sisters or mother or father or children or lands, for my sake and for the gospel, who will not receive a hundredfold now in this time, houses and brothers and sisters and mothers and children and lands, with persecutions, and in the age to come eternal life." (Mark 10:28-30.)

I have always been puzzled by this passage, particularly in connection with the question whether the interpreter is to see an element of humor in it. I doubt that the view is right which denies all elements of a light touch, and I think that somewhere along the line of tradition someone must have had a twinkle in his eye, or maybe a kind of Linus' deadpan expression, when he went on about the "brothers and sisters and mothers and children." At the same time Mark takes the passage seriously, and it points to the present reward for the follower of Christ: here in this present time, in the fellowship of the new community, he gets far, far more than he has given up—with persecutions. But though the emphasis is shifted away from the conclusion "and in the age to come eternal life," it is still there and needs to be there, to give fulfillment to what Mark understood as the essentially temporary character of the situation of historical struggle. The dialectic character of Mark's view of reward comes out even more strongly in the answer to the request for first places made by James and John. Jesus can promise them suffering, but the first place goes to those "for whom it has been prepared" (Mark 10:40), i.e., it cannot be earned by a forward projection of one's own striving. Thus Mark uses a group of traditional passages about reward, and the characteristic emphasis which they receive is that this comes unplanned and, so to speak, unexpectedly.

The motif of *participation* is also present in Mark, quite as fully as in Q. Jesus calls disciples and sends them out with authority (Mark 6:7). They participate, in fact, in his work, and Mark indicates this by giving them the technical term "apostle," authorized delegate, when he recounts their return (Mark 6:30). Their participation includes even their being the vehicles for God's negative judgment—"shake off the dust that is on your feet for a testimony against them" (Mark 6:11). On the other side, "Whoever gives you a cup of water to drink because you bear the name of Christ, will by no means lose his reward" (Mark 9:41). Here, too, compared with Q, it seems that Mark more strongly emphasizes the ambiguity of this par-

ticipation in the work of God through his Christ. For Mark is
continually stressing the imperfectness of the disciples' understanding and obedience—examples are Peter, the disciples
who could not cast out the dumb spirit (Mark 9:14-29) and
those who could not understand about the bread (Mark 8:14-
21). If these passages are to be interpreted in the way that the
Gospel of John presents the disciples' misunderstanding of
Jesus, then this stage of misunderstanding is transcended
when the exalted Christ is present in his community. But this
does not seem to be the intention of Mark. The unflattering
portrait of the disciples is not something from the past, but
something that carries forward into the church. Mark would
have found it difficult to include a saying such as "You, therefore, must be perfect, as your heavenly Father is perfect"
(Matt. 5:48).

Nonetheless, despite their human failings, the disciples are
participating in a work of God. "The gospel must first be
preached to all nations" (Mark 13:10). Thus, as in Q and in
Paul, the disciple is caught up into the eschatological task and
participates in the work that leads to the final fulfillment.

We may note in passing that another type of future appears
in Mark, though only incidentally: "And truly, I say to you,
wherever the gospel is preached in the whole world, what she
has done will be told in memory of her" (Mark 14:9). This
perpetuation of memory in a human future may be implied in
some of the other Marcan sections that at least verge on being
personal legends. The explicit appearance of this motif of con-
tinuance of an act in the human future is a reminder of how
Mark stands at a turning of the ways, and has begun to grapple with the continuing human future as the church had to do.

To summarize: For Mark, the dialectic, that is, the finding
of reality through opposites, is even sharper than in Q. This is
shown by his constant reminder to his readers that the struggle is not over, that the human is always failing, that the present moment calls for renunciation. Mark is very firm in saying
that Christian existence is not that postponement of life to the

future which is often cast as a reproach against Christian faith. Such a stance of faith did exist in early Christianity. It finds clear expression, for instance, in some of the Apocryphal Acts. There are those who find it in Revelation or in Hebrews. But it is not in Mark. Neither does Mark allow his reader to think that the present is already transfigured—a view which could be derived from parts of Q or from John, and which was one of the principal misinterpretations of faith as he understood it that Paul had to contend with. Nonetheless, just as in the case of Q, the phenomenon of faith cannot be confined to the present, for Mark. It reaches powerfully into the future in hope, primarily the hope for the fulfillment of the function of Christ, and into this fulfillment the existence of the believer is drawn, through both the motif of reward and the motif of participation. Though Mark is very anxious to state these motifs in such a way that they will not be misunderstood, it is also inescapably part of his vision of faith that faith participates in and will be drawn into the future which God is creating.

Interpreting Hope in Q and Mark

How important is the kind of hope we see in Q and Mark? What meaning can it have for us today? Most of the attempts to grapple with this question ask directly about the meaning of Christ who is, indeed, central to New Testament faith. Our plan is different: to begin with the roots of hope in sex and creativeness; to see how hope is displaced by the resurgence of an archaic, indefinite infinite, but may be recovered by revising our vision of infinity; and then to move through the themes of secularization and awaiting the end to confront quite directly the structure of hope in a central part of the New Testament. By passing in this way from the most general and biological toward the more specific and historical manifestations of hope, we have tried to show how hope needs a structure to live in, and to make clear what are the kinds of support in the world around that rightly form a "house" for hope. The New Testament is central to this inquiry because it is in the profoundest sense a classic of hope, a place where the depths of man's spirit are released and transformed by the power of hope. It would be very valuable to look further at other varieties of hope perception in the New Testament, particularly at Paul. Instead, we must try, on the basis of our small sampling, to draw some conclusions about how this kind of hope can appear today. We defer the traditional question, the question of Christ, to the final chapter.

HOPE AND PARTICIPATION

The contrast between the Synoptic Gospels and the modern apocalyptic mood is clear enough. Amos Wilder characterizes the fundamental apocalyptic experience, both that of the modern mood and that which lies behind ancient apocalyptic as one of radical disorientation in which there are not merely no answers, but even the categories and the questions have been lost.[12] Both Mark and Q show signs that their kind of faith has passed through such a radical disorientation, but both of these are marked by a sense of having found a new ground, a new house for hope. Such a faith is close enough to the experience of chaos that it can speak to it, but it has, we might say, passed through chaos and come out on the other side. Here lies a good part of the New Testament's place as a classic of hope.

At the same time the faith we have studied fully recognizes the precariousness of the human situation. Along with hope and confidence, it is full of a sense of the fatefulness of decision and of the inability of man to control his whole future. In Mark and Q, it is important to add, the recognition that man is but a tiny part of an immense and mysterious process is not set forth in the deterministic key that is so frequent in apocalyptic. The reality of struggle and the possibility of failure are

clear; in this sense, man's life is still lived in the framework we
set forth above, the framework of the struggle between God
and man.

It is right to say, with most interpreters of the New Testament, that what gives its distinctive profile to the New Testament style of faith and hope is the intensity with which the
goodness of God, the goodness which supports and enables
man's action, is perceived. Forgiveness, grace, justification by
faith, love: these are key terms in the New Testament. They
make a link with a basic theme of process thought, that God
exercises his power by persuasion. Surely the New Testament
does not work this out as a consistent theme, for it does not
acknowledge fully the limitations on God's power that a consistent view of God as the persuader implies. Yet the New
Testament, and particularly the Synoptic Gospels, have
repeatedly opened the way to an existence in freedom and
nonviolence arising from the persuasive and noncompulsive
love of God. For the understanding of hope, however, it is important to move beyond this central insight to see the way in
which Mark and Q enlist the believer to participate in the
movement of the new life into the future.

Christian thought has usually underplayed this theme of
participation, because it has feared that a full recognition of
man's active participation in the movement of life to the future would conflict with the receptiveness by which the new
existence comes to him as a gift. That is why the theme of participation has been emphasized here, for it is an essential one
for the understanding of hope.

To put the question of participating in the coming future
into the framework of our discussion of creativeness, we find
that Christian thinkers have usually been so afraid of making
man's creativeness equal to God's that they have thought of
man's relation to God as almost wholly receptive. It is not accidental that the Synoptic Gospels are secondary to the gospel
of Paul in many theologies, for the elements of free and active
response, and of participation in the coming future, are una-

voidable in them. But Paul too, when he is rightly understood, is not nearly so one-sidedly in favor of receptivity as he is often made to be.[13] And the process perspective can clarify the insight of the Gospel tradition, that man's activity and participation do contribute to the coming future, for in process thinking the future is not determined in advance, but arises from the decisions of actual occasions as they come to be and aim toward their relevant future.

For our interpretation of this hope, it is most important to see that in the hope of Mark and Q, what transforms the ego-projecting strivings, the relevant future simply as the projection of self, into the giving of oneself into a larger reality, is not simply the sense of receiving new life as a gift, but equally the sense of being enlisted in a task that will constitute the future. From the eschatological vocation of the early Christians, a long line runs through Puritanism to our American sense of righteous purpose in building a better world—a reminder of the varied meanings a given form of belief may take. We are today so disillusioned with our American dream that we are suspicious of the whole vision of participating in the future. Besides, the chaotic nature of our present history makes us despair of finding continuity of purpose in it.

Nevertheless, despite its perversion and its erosion, hope that is not just passive, but involves enlistment in the future, is the basic form of hope which the Christian tradition can offer to the present world. The paradigm of hope that we found in Mark and Q can still be a forward-looking pattern in which men live. Today we see that the final end toward which hope reaches will have to be transformed, in our grasp of it, into an endless movement into the future, as we showed in the previous chapter. The new life for which one hopes will never come to be the prevalent reality in a total way, though real changes and achievements are possible. If we think otherwise, the end will become either an excuse for otherworldliness or else a symbol of the indefinite totality that swallows up all concrete reality. Further, a modern man cannot live in this hope with the unreflective security which has sometimes marked Christian faith. Hope will be real on the boundary between hope and despair.

But when all this is said, the hope we sketched remains a viable hope. For it to be so, we must believe that some real possibility lies ahead. To clarify how this can be, we now turn to the theme of eternal life.

VII
Eternal Life

The previous two chapters have shown that the hope for the end does not express an unrelieved longing for perfection, but that it embodies also the elements of fulfillment and participation which give this hope a processive character and make it possible to interpret it in a process framework. We now turn to the hope for eternal life, the hope that the individual's existence will not be lost, but will be taken up into and contribute to the future.

It is often said that hope for eternal life has little to do with eschatology as hope for the final end. Those who say this see eternal life as an escape into a timeless realm, and regard the hope for eternal life as individualistic and legalistic, a matter of rewards and punishments. At the same time, the identical limitation of excessive individualism is a feature of much of the current interpretation of eschatology. For a widespread way of making eschatology meaningful in our time is to point to the moment of personal decision as the existential "weight" of the hope for the end. Our own study of the hope for the end has paralleled this existentialist interpretation to the extent that it also reinterprets the symbol of a final summing up, and rejects the notion of a predetermined or final total meaning of history. But we tried to show that the elements of historical continuity, of men taking part in the work and purpose of God, and of cumulative enrichment of the resources of the present, can still be meaningful without the belief in a single and unifying end—even though neither the secularized idea of progress nor the traditional idea of sacred history can be held any longer.

Though the hope for eternal life is commonly held to be either crudely legalistic or strongly nontemporal, we shall show that the same hope for cumulative participation and for the fulfillment of one's contribution are actually central motivating factors in the hope for eternal life, and we shall try to show how they can be made meaningful by a process interpretation.

ETERNAL LIFE AND THE VALUATION OF THE HUMAN

Today it is common to think that by turning away from belief in eternal life, men are better able to see the value of actual existence here and now. Exactly the opposite seems to be the case! The loss of a vision of the eternal dimension of life has gone hand in hand with a fearful shrinking of what we may call the imagined dimensions of life here and now. And a massive disregard for the value of human life still persists to belie the claim that men have been freed for each other by turning away from the otherworldliness of belief in eternal life. The study of secularization in Chapter IV showed that the shift of focus toward the secular has to be challenged and rethought by any point of view that intends to stand in continuity with Christian faith, even though many aspects of secularization are inevitable and many are also in harmony with the intention of faith. The rejection or ignoring of the hope for eternal life is part of the move toward secularization, and it needs to be challenged precisely because it is not humanizing or liberating, but produces a flattened and devitalized vision of the possibilities of human existence.

Most men who live without any vision of how life reaches beyond the moment lose respect for themselves and also lose the capacity to give themselves to others. It is one of the great ironies of the present situation that the isolation of the person within himself and in the moment is so often presented as if it liberated men for concern and caring, for a sense of the immense treasure of the other's life and for an openness to the worth of existence generally. One deeply respects the heroic humanism of those who do find openness to their neighbor in a vision that resolutely denies any continuing effects to human encounter. If that is the way things are, one has to face it and live with it. More than that, the criticisms of the old faith as escapist have real substance. This book also renounces the idea that faith operates in a separate realm, and sees God and faith as meaningful only when understood as interacting with the world.

Nevertheless, the whole modern critique of traditional Christian faith in eternal life as otherworldly is a twisted one. For the conviction that belief in eternal life is escapist is a misreading of how traditional Christian faith has actually functioned, and a result of the narrowing of the vision of life to center it on oneself. It is only when eternal life becomes merely a question of "my" eternal life that it is subject to the common criticism of legalism and escapism. The conventional modern critique of this hope makes eternal life simply a matter of one's preoccupation with oneself—a longing for an indefinite prolongation of one's own existence. Beyond this, many more sophisticated critics have inferred that eternal life plays the role in religious experience of assuring an even balance of justice through the belief in rewards and punishments in heaven and hell.

If these were the central issues, the criticism would be a strong and valid one. No doubt many Christians have wanted eternal life to be a mere prolongation of their existence and have also hoped for the evening out of rewards and penalties in the afterlife. Eternal life as evasion of death is apparent enough in the contemporary world, for instance in the development of "cryonics," the freezing of the corpse in the hope of later revivification, and a few even dare to visualize the medical elimination of physical death.[1] The literature of such movements shows a pathetically paranoid tendency, and there is no doubt that within the Christian tradition there have been many who were equally escapist and who refused to face the reality of their limitation. Nevertheless, the definition of eternal life as self-projection simply has not paid attention to the actual concerns of those who believe in eternal life.

ACCEPTANCE OF DEATH

In the setting of faith, what is at stake is very different. In the first place, we agree with the critics that acceptance of death is part of acceptance of responsibility in the present moment. The definiteness of the moment is inescapably connected with its transience and thus with the realization that existence is existence toward death (Heidegger). Actual living does not permit the indefinite postponement of decision that is symbolized by the unreality of death or by the indefinite continuation of the present life.

But "existence toward death" is not the only way in which the definiteness of present reality may be grasped. In a well-known essay Bultmann has compared Heidegger's "existence toward death" with "existence toward the neighbor" (Gogarten), as an even more concrete presentation of the definiteness and decision-character of the moment.[2] Here love, which means acknowledging the neighbor rather than death as the definite limitation of existence, is the center of concreteness and limitation. Love is made possible by the antecedent love that sets us free to live by and for the "limitation" of the neighbor. In the final chapter we shall return to the question of how sharply the antecedent love, the love that precedes and enables our love, has to be understood in connection with the message about Christ (as Bultmann takes it), and how far it can be understood, like existence toward death, as a general human possibility. For the time being we leave this question open in order to concentrate on the point that Christian faith makes a clear connection between love and death, and knows that life and love are paradoxically made possible only by giving oneself up. This connection is especially drawn out in the symbolism of the cross; it has been powerfully expressed by Bultmann in the essay referred to. The note of loss of self in a larger reality connects this joining of love and death with the romantic union of love and death noted in Chapter I. Though both of these share the motif of sacrifice, however, they are quite different in this, that the romantic union of love and death sees the two coming together in a "totality" in which there is loss of all concrete distinctions, while the joining of love and death that is free from romantic longing and is simply open to the reality of the other, sharpens attention to the momentary and concrete instead of leading toward a loss of the definite in an infinite totality.

According to Bultmann, the man who is set free for responsible existence in this way is by that very fact set free from the fear of death, so that the question of death no longer concerns him. Of course he does not mean that so complete a freedom from concern about death is ordinarily actually achieved. Yet insofar as one is really open to and thereby limited by the other, he is already free from the fear of death by the very acceptance of his being limited. But so far we have seen little about the future. Bultmann's presentation concentrates on the other or neighbor as encountered in the moment. This way of looking at the question comes from Bultmann's fear that if the future beyond the moment can be known or visualized, it will come to be under man's control and will thus become again, despite the concern for the neighbor, a field for self-projection and control. Hence, Bultmann affirms that faith brings one into life rather than death, but he refuses to express "life" except as a momentary encounter.

Bultmann, here following Paul, has done well to emphasize the dubious and egocentric possibilities of descriptions of the future. Acceptance of limitation, and thus of death, is the only route to freedom and health. This was a major theme of hope in Mark and Q, presented in the previous chapter. At the same time it cannot be said that the widespread loss of faith in eternal life has been accompanied by a significant increase in acceptance of responsibility for the neighbor or for the present moment. Part of the reason lies in the lack of clarity about what we mean by the present moment. Responsibility entails consequences in the future, and the "pure present" is most fully found in experiences that involve disorientation to time and thus to responsibility. A decision taken strictly in the moment is an unrelated decision. The very concept of decision, or of love as acting, involves relation both to the ongoing reality of the self which makes the decision and to the ongoing reality of that person or situation for which the decision is made.

The restrictive and irresponsible result of concentrating on the present moment in decision is apparent in many ways. It is one of the typically modern attempts to empty the continuing process of life of its depth and richness. We will cite only one example: the tendency toward fanaticism that inheres in preoccupation with the present moment. If one is unable to see the crisis of decision in a larger framework, he will easily be pressed into a fanatic posture. The fanaticism of revolutionary movements is closely related to their fear that this moment is the only moment. In this way concentration on the moment becomes an evasion of death.

At this point Martin Buber has much to teach those who explore the "moment of encounter," for Buber's faith enabled him both to stress engagement with the present moment and to tolerate failure. Confronting and accepting death, as Buber saw and as Christian faith has also seen by putting together the symbols of death and resurrection, does not mean confronting a void or a total annihilation. Reality and history are not exhausted in the moment. Death may be honestly confronted at the same time that something more is recognized.

The Future as the Other's Future

The future and the life that we are able to grasp in connection with our own death is the other's future. Thus we have to go a step beyond concern for the other in the moment, and recognize that if he is to be taken seriously, his future is of real concern. Concern about eternal life in Christian faith is not so much a matter of one's own future as it is a concern for the other's future. Freedom to take another's existence seriously is grounded in the faith that his future is of serious meaning. It may not have been so in every epoch, but there is a sense in which, at least in our own time, our *own* future is opaque in a way that the other's is not. Gabriel Marcel goes to the heart of the matter when he says that love means refusing to give the other over to death. "To love a being is to say, 'Thou shalt not die.'"[3] It is true that such concern for the other's future is not as free from a real kind of self-concern as it seems to be in the actual moments of intense awareness of the other's existence as of inexpressible value. We noted in Chapter I how the child becomes a symbol of hope initially as a projection of the parent's existence. The transformation of this relation of hope into a deep concern for the other does not eliminate the element of self-fulfillment in the future of the other. Why should it? As long as this future does not become our "product" which we try to control, there is no reason to deny, as some have tried to do, that we find ourselves fulfilled in our hope for the other. Even from the point of view of the self-transcendence of Christian faith, there remains a real element of self-activity in concern for the other's future. But this concern is transformed so that it goes beyond the desire to control, and grants freedom to the other.

DEATH, WASTE, AND THE FUTURE

Love as openness to the other's future does not mean blindness to waste and loss, nor is it a concern about the just measure of reward and punishment. At the beginning of this book we noted the tension between biological self-transcendence in the creation of and care for a child, on the one hand, and the immense waste of the reproductive and evolutionary processes on the other. In analyzing expectation of the end, we saw a very similar tension in the eschatological vision, between the hoped-for future fulfillment and the immense waste of history. This tension between hope and waste comes to focus in the question of death and eternal life. The acceptance of death means the acceptance, not just of one's own death, but of the incalculable waste and tragedy of history, even though this waste is one which we can neither fully realize nor bear. The affirmation of eternal life means that over against waste and tragedy there is, in spite of all, a renewing power at work. If it is true that many sensitive modern people do not find evidence that a renewing power is at work, we hold that a genuine part, at least, of the reason lies in the outmoded notion of infinity which we discussed in Chapter III: imaginations which have been shaped by the image of a God who is in total control are honest in saying that they do not find that the world is compatible with such a God. But once we are free from this discredited view, our minds can be much more open to the evidences for a divine persuasion that reopens possibilities, lures toward higher intensities, and more loving action, and counteracts while accepting the waste, tragedy, and death which are so evident. And once our minds are free from this older notion of God, we can see much more readily what was at stake in the traditional hope for eternal life: the movement of life and meaning into the future, which grasps us as the future of the other.

We shall explore the meaning of this hope in three aspects: eternal life as contribution to the culture; as everlasting valuation and remembering by God; and as the actual renewal of the self after death.

ETERNAL LIFE AS CONTRIBUTION TO THE CULTURE

In the first place, one who has faith in eternal life expresses a sense of belonging to a larger reality, a reality which contributes to his life and which receives the contribution of his life. Such a faith arose in a much more stable and traditional culture than our own, a culture in which it could be assumed without reflection that the existence and effort of the self were taken up into the ongoing life of the group and culture. A practical and this-worldly sense has always been the first level of meaning conveyed by the imagery of eternal life. The child who carries forward the life of the parent—a figure which has been central to our whole reflection about hope—is thus the initial symbol of eternal life.

In earlier times, most forms of belief in the survival of the self were closely linked to the way in which the self was thought to keep on being effective in the group. In some cultures, as among the Hebrews who were so important in shaping our own sensibility, a direct concern for social and cultural immortality all but blocked out the archaic belief in the survival of the self. What they cared about was the continuation of their life in the community. What we have called the problem of waste was keenly felt, but it was overcome by the strong participation in the life and hope of the community. The erosion of this earlier sense of participation in the hope of the community does not need to be documented. Many speak of it as something now irretrievably gone. At the same time special groups in our society still have the power to give meaning to the lives of their members by giving them a sense of participating in the future. This is especially the case of protesting and revolutionary groups. The fragile character of such hope is shown, of course, by the fluctuating and unpredictable life of these groups. On the other hand, the passion they arouse discloses how deeply the need to belong to the future is built into our imagination. Less intense, but in many ways similar to the revolutionary quest for identity is the nationalist quest for identity which has power precisely because it assures the individual that he takes part in a continuing existence.

Thus though much of our philosophy and art explores the possibility of isolated, individual existence, the power of the longing to be a part of a larger whole which reaches into the future is forcefully evident in many ways. A thoughtful American Jew may well say, as one said to me, that he would give up his Jewish identity if the State of Israel should cease to exist. Coming from a sensitive member of the community whose future has been most harshly threatened in our time, such a comment discloses how necessary to us our corporate future remains.

Most of the standard treatments of the history of Christian faith downplay this element in it. They are afraid, as we saw in studying the Synoptic Gospels, that any emphasis on man's participation in his community's future will be a relapse into "good works," and a threat to the receptivity of faith. But it would be hard to find a religion that has inspired a stronger sense of vocation to participate in and contribute to the growth of an actual community. Paul, Augustine, medieval monasticism, Luther, Puritanism—all in their various ways were powerful exemplifications of this primary way of relating to the future.

At the same time, we have seen so much of a perverted and demonic attempt to control the future that many today think it much safer just to live in the present. What distinguishes a healthy participation in the group from one that is perverted by an uncritical and aggressive self-projection? We have already noted one test: the acceptance of death can free one to live freely toward the future. But the acceptance of death and a deep concern for the other require that the future be open and trustworthy even when the social future is chaotic. Men feel the claim of responsibility and of creativeness in a depth that requires more than a social and historical future. Thus we turn to the second dimension of eternal life: eternal life in the memory of God.

ETERNAL LIFE AS GOD'S MEMORY

A thoughtful reader will be impressed by the variety of sensitive modern minds who have expressed in one way or another a vision of life and its effects transcending the moment and the social context. The Eastern motif of reincarnation—

the reappearance of the soul in successive lives—is a way of expressing such a faith that reaches far beyond the growing circles of those who are learning to participate directly in Eastern religion. The Soviet poet and essayist, Valentin Kataev, uses reincarnation as at least a symbol of that in life which reaches beyond matter.[4] For those who are interested in the theology of the future, it is more noteworthy that another Marxist, Ernst Bloch, who later became a great interpreter of hope, as a young man wrote very seriously about the transmigration of souls. So strong was his sense that an individual life was too fragmentary to be a unit of meaning that he brought into his thinking the idea that the soul has many lives.[5] His essay is a strong testimony to the fact that the thrust of life to reach to a beyond is not escapist.

Nikos Kazantzakis grasps it differently, and speaks of man building God, or of man saving God. Kazantzakis' imagination was strongly turned toward the future:

Which is that one force amid all of God's forces which man is able to grasp? Only this: we discern a crimson line on this earth, a red, blood-spattered line which ascends, struggling, from matter to plants, from plants to animals, from animals to men. . . . Difficult, dreadful, unending ascension.[6]

Fully to explore the vision of Kazantzakis would be a major task in itself, but we note his vision of an unending future, of a God who is not "in control," but is playful and ecstatic rather than legal and determining, and finally, his conviction that man contributes to God or helps to build God. All this in Kazantzakis is in anguished counterpoint with the themes of death and loss, but nonetheless his is a powerful testimony from a profound poetic visionary of how eternal life reaches beyond the isolated individual and beyond the empirical society to a transcendent dimension.

Far better known to those who are concerned with the theology of the future is Teilhard de Chardin.[7] His vision of an Omega point, a point of unifying convergence toward which life and history are struggling, remains one of the most fundamental options in the theology of hope. Teilhard brought into focus most of the real questions for such a theology. He did not believe that solid hope could be sustained by a subjective theology; he oriented his speculative vision toward a reengagement of the church with the world; he saw that hope pointed ever beyond its short-term goals to a "beyond" that he called an Absolute. Seeing that an Absolute to which the individual in his inwardness could relate was not enough to claim the faith of men seriously engaged in a changing, processive reality, he projected the Absolute into the future. Teilhard's work is a real recovery of the eschatological dimension of Christian faith, and it serves as well to make a large sector of this eschatological vision accessible to men outside the church. Nevertheless, Teilhard was not radical and novel enough in reconceptualizing the Absolute toward which his faith tended. In one sense, God is deeply involved in time for Teilhard, for Christ is a power of growth in the world. But the discomfort of Teilhard with the possibility of failure, as well as his view that man must have been intended by evolution from the beginning, show that he has not fully opened his Absolute to the interactiveness of events in time. His vision of the Omega point as a point of intensified human love and mutuality, so intense and real that it can survive or rise above the decay of the physical universe, was his way of showing how hope reaches beyond the sociohistorical context. But if real freedom is a property of acts at every level of complexity, a fixed, single point of convergence is not an appropriate aim for God; the goal will have to be modified according to the actual acts that take place. Grateful as we are to Teilhard, his notion of the Absolute is subject to many of the criticisms we have made above of the traditional Christian absolute.

A very different thinker, the Jewish philosopher Hans Jonas, critical student of Heidegger and of modern biology, has come to the conclusion that successive lives enrich the sustaining reality, the ultimate God. Despite his criticisms of Whitehead on other grounds, Jonas comes very close to Whitehead's understanding of the way in which actual occasions are taken account of by God in his consequent nature. Jonas grounds his view in the fact that "in moments of decision, when our whole being is involved, we feel as if acting under the eyes of eternity." "Not the agents," he says, "which must ever pass, but their acts enter into the becoming godhead and indelibly form his never decided image." [8] We note here the image of building God which also appears in Kazantzakis.

Whitehead's way of giving an account of the sense that things matter in some eternal way has already been set forth, and it is the way of giving form to this intuition which is chosen here. As he puts it in an essay on immortality, "realization is an essential factor in the world of value," [9] and realization in the concrete world must find its counterpart in God. In his consequent nature, God constantly receives each occasion as it occurs at its proper rank and retains it everlastingly. Over against the loss and "waste" in the process of the coming to be and ceasing of actual occasions, and the tragic course of history, here there is a preservation of what is worth preserving. It is the confidence that in spite of the waste in the world, the occasions which pass are recognized everlastingly in God and not lost that gives an ultimate ground to hope in a process perspective.

Such a view recognizes the element of God's taking each concrete occasion seriously, a characteristic that we noted was also an aspect of apocalyptic hope. There is a kinship here with the widespread mystical view that everything returns to God, but the difference is that here the return to God does not mean a reabsorption into the undifferentiated infinite. For God is involved in time, and his existence is enriched. This makes a point of contact with the language of both Kazantzakis and Jonas, who speak boldly of man "building" God. We would rather say, man contributes to God, but the bolder phrase is right in saying that God is changed by what happens in the world.[10]

ETERNAL LIFE AS THE RENEWAL OF PERSONAL EXISTENCE

Immortality in God's memory is a powerful basis for hope, one that confers on man's life a sense of participating in the future and makes it possible to accept the defeat of specific historical hopes without despair. Yet the human experience of hope is so deeply engaged in the interactive, dynamic movement of personal existence into the future that traditional religious hope has gone on to affirm the renewal of the self to life beyond death. And while this faith has by no means been uniquely Christian, it has been central to Christian hope through the years.

We can only remark in passing that the debates among theologians about the merits of "immortality" versus "resurrection" as ways of thinking about the hope for the renewal of the self are not really central to a modern grappling with the problem of hope. If there is reality in the hope for a new life, the reality appears in both ways of conceiving it, and yet neither the traditional immortality nor the traditional resurrection is an adequate framework for thinking about it. For the traditional "immortality" was too much bound to a dualistic separation of soul and body, and the traditional "resurrection" was too much bound to the image of a final end which we have rejected. If we are to take this hope seriously, we shall have to develop ways of thinking about it which are not narrowly bound to either of these traditional ways.

Instead of looking further into this history of Christian thinking about the future life, however, it is more important to press forward and note the objections which have been raised against this form of hope, since so much contemporary Christian thought joins with most secular thought in denying that eternal life is either possible or desirable.

Those who deny that we should hope for a new life beyond death argue that such a faith is just an egocentric self-projection into the future. Some of our most distinguished theologians have taken this stand. Surely they are right that

Christians and religious people generally have often used this kind of hope as an egocentric way of escaping both from their own difficulties and from the claims that other people made upon them. But we have tried to show, both in our presentation of hope in Mark and Q, and in the first part of this chapter, that hope for eternal life is—more profoundly than a mere self-projection—a hope that appears through and beyond the acceptance of death, as an affirmation of the reality and trustworthiness of the unrealized future and especially the future of the other, which is in God's hands. If men such as Hartshorne and Tillich have belittled the hope for a renewal of personal existence after death, they have been right in criticising some of its shallower forms, but they have nonetheless failed to see the deeper reaches of this hope.[11] As a result they, like many other thinkers, have failed to inquire forcibly into the possibility of life after death.

What, then, of the possibility of the renewal of the self to life after death? We dare to ask the question because we believe that the process perspective which we follow has reopened this question in a very significant way. For if consciousness is completely dependent on the physical organism, it is clear that when the physical organism ceases to exist, consciousness will also cease. We know that our conscious selves are profoundly constituted by the physical bodies with which they interact, and we know as well that this dependence is more far-reaching than we are now able to specify. To take one instance, and one that is central for the continuity of the self, memory is dependent on some physiological process of storage in the brain—a truth that is sharply driven home by those experiments which show that brain cells from an animal which has learned a given procedure, when eaten by or injected into another animal, will in certain cases enable it to learn the procedure more quickly. But it is by no means evident at present that memory is totally dependent on computerlike storage in the brain. This example shows how our thinking must remain open to our growing knowledge as it develops. But it is equally true that our knowledge will never be complete, and that we are far less like computers than a schematic sketch of memory would suggest. It is extremely important that we do not come to understand ourselves simply by projecting forward the tendencies of a particular scientific theory, but also bring into our picture the actual experiences of freedom, creativeness, responsibility, and interactive encounter which we have.

The very way in which Whitehead's philosophy brings these two requirements together opens the way for a fresh look at the question of life after death. John B. Cobb, Jr., has explored this area most fully. He shows how Whitehead's categories provide an understanding of the self as more than a complex psychophysical organism. In a complex living being such as man there is reason to posit a series of presiding occasions through which the organism achieves central control. These occasions have continuity in time as a series of occasions, a "living person," or "soul." [12] By combining endurance and life the presence of a soul makes possible a peculiar richness and intensity of experience. There is, then, in men not merely the psychophysical organization of high degree, but a dominant series of occasions characterized by their serial prehension of each other, though also profoundly interacting with the occasions in the brain. Such a view would open the possibility that such a living person or soul could exist in another environment than that of the human body and specifically the brain.

Cobb's discussion is amply rewarding in its own right, and the reader who wishes to follow further the details of how a process concept of the self takes account both of the self's dependence on the body and of its uniqueness is referred to his analysis.[13] Here we can only clarify two points that are important for our purpose.

In the first place, the use of the term "soul" does not mean that we are back again in a dualistic framework of thinking. The actual occasions which, taken as a series, make up the presiding center of the person are at bottom constituted in the same way as other occasions. It is true that the extremely complex and intense feelings that a human self is able to experience are conceivable by us only in terms of the bodily experience which now sustains the soul. It is also true that the only ground for believing that this fragile and dependent center of experience could exist apart from the body would be the conviction that the life and experience of such souls was of importance to God. The Whiteheadian framework gives us a way of understanding the soul as a distinct center of freedom in the person. A conviction of faith would be the only basis for saying that such souls could continue, or be renewed to existence, after the death of the body. Furthermore, though there is no theoretical reason why such souls might not communicate with embodied souls, it is our judgment that the evidence for such communication is extremely unconvincing. In this sense the life after death is a separate realm—it is, let us say, one that we are too insensitive to respond to. The contrary view leads to the acceptance of what are clearly wish projections as real interpersonal communication.[14]

In the second place, the view developed here does show how an existence after death could be freed from the intense competitiveness that is a mark of biological life. For life depends upon food; the increase of energy in a biologically living system requires a constant input of energy, and biologically living organisms have to "feed" on less intensely organized energy systems. Biological life must thus be an island of concentrated energy in a universe in which energy tends to dissipate and run down. But this characteristic of physically observed energy is not necessarily a property of all actual occasions. Just as we suppose that something analogous to memory is a property of God, though he does not depend on any computerlike memory-storage system, so we suppose that God interacts with the world without being threatened by loss of energy. Similarly, souls existing apart from bodies might prehend the occasions of each other's experience without the concentration of energy that is necessary for a biological organism. Something like this is what Teilhard de Chardin had in mind when he wrote of his belief that when evolution and history had brought radial energy (his term for the "internal" energy of events) to a sufficiently intense level, the latter would be able to sustain itself and its relations without the base of "tangential energy" (his term for measurable physical energy) which originally enabled it to reach such a level of concentration.[15] Whitehead does not reflect on this problem in these terms, for he did not explore this kind of immortality, instead giving his attention to the immortality in the memory of God discussed above. But in an important passage he suggests his awareness of something very similar, when he says, "The everlasting nature of God, which in a sense is nontemporal and in another sense is temporal, may establish with the soul a peculiarly intense relationship of mutual immanence. Thus in some important sense the existence of the soul may be freed from its complete dependence on the bodily organization." [16]

Can we suppose that a finite center of experience is capable of infinite possibilities of new experience? For there is no reason to hope for a static future life. This is a serious question. But it will not do to settle it by simply contrasting the infinite God with finite selves or souls. A major thrust of our discussion of infinity was to show that infinity as a symbol of God tends to obscure the concern of God with the concrete and definite that is so central a concern of Christian faith and is also characteristic of Whitehead. In contrast to certain absolute notions of infinity, the God of process thought is already limited, yet he is capable of the realization of infinite possibilities. Holding strongly to the distinction between God and man, it is not wrong to hold that definite and limited centers of experience, such as human souls, may be, in interaction with one another and with God, capable of the realization of an infinitely expanding horizon of possibilities, so that one does not need to exclude a hope for eternal life on the ground that it would necessarily lead to boredom.

In conclusion, it must be emphasized that such a hope is not a hope for utopian perfection. In the first place, since it is hope grounded in faith, it must be hope that leaves in God's hands the decision about what is finally worth preserving. Furthermore, it is a hope which does not try to say that there is no real loss in the waste and tragedy of the existence that we now know. Nor will it expect to cast off the imperfections and failures of this life painlessly, even though it will not be primarily concerned with balancing rewards and punishments. It does not follow that life after death will be "pie in the sky." Neither does it follow that such a new kind of existence will be free from the possibility of wrong choices.

Nevertheless, the reach of hope into the future, not for static perfection, but for new possibilities of interaction and creativeness, is profoundly met in faith by the sense that God supports this reach into the future. Little as we can imagine it, eternal life as renewal of the soul after death is a valid hope in our time and one which can and will reinforce the more short-range hope that is so essential for human survival.

In so saying, we have come a long way from the hope that is biologically expressed in the child. Our thought has moved steadily from the socially visible dimensions of hope toward those aspects of it which are most specially and characteristically bound up with the experience of God or of the "beyond." We have already seen that though some forms of experience of God are quite diffusely present in our world today, they are forms of experience that deemphasize the concern of God for the concrete and definite, and point toward the dissolution of the definite in the undifferentiated. The style characteristic of Christian faith, however, points in the other direction, toward the value and meaning of the definite foci of experience. If faith such as we have sketched above is to be viable, it will have to draw from the Christian experience of Christ, which leads beyond itself toward the God who cares for the definite foci of experience, the selves who interact with him.

VIII
Christ and Jesus

THE FORMAL STRUCTURE OF THE FIGURE OF CHRIST

In the previous chapters we have first set forth a structure of existence within which hope can live—a "house for hope"—and then have shown how process categories can clarify such a structure and show its relation to other aspects of what we know. Here we shall follow the opposite course, and first set forth a theoretical description of Christ in process categories, and then show how such a reality, so described, can be relevant to hope. As will appear, this order will put first the aspect which is most repugnant to traditional doctrine; after that is squarely faced, the ways in which this process view of Christ can fulfill the hopes of other Christologies can better be judged.

The reality known as the living Christ is an extremely complex one, and it is rash to oversimplify. Nonetheless we make bold to say: Christ is a concrete possibility, that is, in Whiteheadian language, a proposition or theory. This means that Christ is not an actual entity, but has reality, like all propositions, as a hybrid between actual entities and pure potentials or possibilities. "Propositions," in Whitehead's system, are the principal lures to higher attainment in the more complex actual occasions. They have various functions. Here we concentrate on one: they are "sentences" that link the wholly abstract entities (pure potentials or "eternal objects") which are the predicates of the propositions with actual occasions that may become the subjects. A proposition expresses a concrete possibility. As such, propositions may be lures to greater complexity in a rich variety of ways. One of the most important of these, and the particular function of the proposition on which we need to focus, is that a proposition may suggest a certain way in which an actual occasion may actualize itself or an aspect of itself. In other words, the subjective aim of an occasion is a propositional feeling, a prehension of a proposition which has the occasion itself as its subject and a particular cluster of eternal objects as predicate.

This is precisely the function of Christ in faith. The "figure" of Christ expresses a concrete possibility which is a lure or challenge to realization in the actual human existences to which this proposition or symbol is presented. Of course this is a very general definition; the figure of Christ shares this function with an infinite number of possibilities. And Christ is a general proposition that takes innumerable specific forms. Nor is it the case that the figure of Christ appears only in a proposition related to the subjective aim of an occasion in the life of a person. Clearly this figure may also be perceived in more "distant" ways—in history, in relation to other lives than one's own, etc. Nevertheless, the central function of the figure of Christ, and the key to its surprising power, is disclosed by the definition here proposed.

This definition has the merit (which some may regard as a weakness) of telescoping moral demand and aesthetic appeal. The call or claim of Christ is as much aesthetic as it is moral, a fact which can be seen all the more clearly if we consider that the actual meeting with this concrete possibility takes place as often through the impact of some life which partly embodies it, or through some modern literary or symbolic form, as it does with the traditional explicit figure of Christ. Such a telescoping of the moral and aesthetic dimensions in this realm has been rejected by much contemporary theology because some

of the earlier liberalism sentimentalized the aesthetic appeal
of the "beauty" of Christ. But this deterioration of the aesthetic dimension must not obscure a fundamental point: that
(to put it in traditional language) one who proclaims the
Christian faith is a poet, creating a convincing world of vision
with the figure of Christ at its center, rather than one who is
simply making a moral appeal. The moral appeal view of com-
municating the Christian faith presupposes that men already
have the standard of judgment by which to recognize that
they ought to respond, whereas the poet is actually creating a
world in which the response can be meaningful; he calls for a
shift or change in the standards themselves. A great deal of
the recent study of the language of faith and of the "linguisti-
cality of reality" has been making a point similar to this; we
apply it directly to Christ.

The formal pattern of such a Christology has its historical
roots with Arius and William Ellery Channing rather than
with the mainstream of Protestant or Catholic orthodoxy. It
has in common with them the insight that the traditional ways
of interpreting Christ, in their effort to grasp his uniqueness,
have so much isolated Christ from the cultural reality in
which men live that the figure of Christ is in danger of losing
all relevance. The reduction of the ontological status of Christ
to the level of a proposition or concrete possibility also has in
common with its unorthodox predecessors the risk of losing
what is distinctive in the effort to be meaningful. But the history of theology shows that it is better to take a risk than to be
safe, and there is far more to be lost by refusing to try the new
than by making mistakes.

To one who protests, "Is that all there is to Christ?" one can
say emphatically that whatever is, is. Reality, in the last analysis, can take care of itself. Just because we have such a confidence that what is real will in the long run show itself to be
real, we can confidently explore our interpretation of it. But
even this is not the whole story. Reality is not just what it is; it
is also what it becomes. If Christ is a concrete possibility or

proposition, this possibility has no importance unless men try to make it actual. In the larger setting of this book, it is hoped that the view of Christ here developed can make a positive contribution to this end.

If a process Christology of Christ as a proposition or concrete possibility ruthlessly reduces Christ to an intermediate or hybrid level of reality, to the status in fact of an aesthetic object, this approach has two great merits in relation to the current efforts to understand faith. First, on the side of the relation between faith and culture, it is an asset to realize that the reality of Christ has so much in common with other "concrete possibilities," or, to shift the language, symbolic forms. The immense suggestiveness of the recent writing on how to interpret earlier forms of the Christian faith (the so-called "new hermeneutic") arises from the fact that it draws on modes of interpreting other concrete possibilities or imagined forms of possible worlds. The "later Heidegger" had been concerned to understand how to interpret a poem. The theologians of the new hermeneutic have used Heidegger's model to interpret Christ and Christian language. Their work is widely recognized as among the most important theological advances of today. It works, it fits its subject matter, because in a very important sense Christ *is* a poem. These brief remarks will have to serve to relate the perspective developed here to this important theological movement.

Second, and here our perspective moves beyond much of the interpretation focused on language, to take the figure of Christ as a proposition, or reality hybrid between actuality and potentiality, has the tremendous advantage of clarifying Christ's function as mediator. God and men are the actual occasions to which the proposition is relevant; or, more exactly, God and men are personally ordered series of actual occasions. The reduction in the level of existence of the Christ figure is the correlative of taking God with utter seriousness as an actual and effective reality, instead of banishing him to the periphery as is so often done today. This view purposely runs counter to the tendency of so much Christology today, to make Christ bear the whole weight of meaning once attributed to God. That is more than the figure of Christ can do. On the contrary, Christ's function is to mediate between God and man, to make it possible for men to respond more fully to the purpose of God. This is not a function applying uniquely to Christ. All propositions are lures to some kind of complexity, and the actuality of complex and intense experience is God's aim. Whitehead himself happens to illustrate the function of propositions by the use of two fully verbal propositions, Hamlet's famous speech and the sayings in the Gospels.[1] Further, most propositions function below the level of consciousness (so, often, does the figure of Christ!). Even in conscious response, the relation between the proposition as a stimulus to novel action and God as the ultimate source of that stimulus remains unconscious or vague in most cases. It is also clear from contemporary theology that the concrete possibility which we call Christ can still function very effectively for a time when separated in consciousness from God. Nevertheless, we maintain that so far as the human situation is concerned, the kind of response that is called for by the figure of Christ is one in which, in the process of clarification, the proposition points beyond itself to its source, God himself. Other propositions may do this too. Our sense of the reality of God would be thin indeed if they could not. It is worth emphasizing that though men may become conscious of God through various aspects of their relation to him, the distinctively Christian emphasis in knowledge of God is connected with God as the one who leads to the future through persuading toward a certain kind of concrete possibility. But the special character of the figure of Christ is that it both points impellingly toward concrete human existence, and is open toward the equally concrete reality of God. Although no complex symbol or proposition can be fully clarified (if it is powerful, it will have an aura of suggested meanings that interwork in unimaginably complex ways), we shall try to clarify how this double direction of the figure of Christ works.[2]

THE EMBODIMENT OF THE CONCRETE POSSIBILITY

The figure of Christ is hopeful only so long as it has, or has prospect of, embodiment in actual people. But it is also the nature of this possibility that it continually eludes complete expression or embodiment. The proposed predicate is never fully expressed by the concrescing subjects. In bringing it to expression, those who respond to it always eliminate some aspects of the proposition in order to bring it into harmony with other competing propositions which they are also bent on expressing. In the life that is grasped by it, the embodiment of the figure of Christ is always a compromised one. For this reason, there is a real problem in identifying the proposition; it transcends all its concrete expressions. Whether or not this was also the case with Jesus is a question to which we shall have to return. In a weak sense any complex proposition transcends any of its expressions or embodiments. There is no perfect performance of a symphony, and a performance that is shaped to bring out one side of its pattern is forced to underplay another. But the figure of Christ is a symbol of which this transcendence of the actual embodying occasion is decisive and also problematic, both because this figure claims to bring God close and because the claim or lure to embodiment is so impelling.

Yet the center of the disclosure of God by Christ is the power of this figure to set the one who is grasped by it in a framework of acceptance, of opening him to the continuing gift of new life. It is the power of acceptance that makes the impossible claim bearable. This figure does not merely call for expression of itself, but points beyond itself to the concrete source of giving, to God himself. If the function of opening men to the reality from which we receive is neglected, and Christ is presented simply as a paradigm of full humanness, the figure will soon be exhausted of its power. It is the confidence that a process perspective can help us to see that this sustaining and forgiving factor is a real part of our total inter-

active situation, and not just a projection of our wishes, that
makes us propose this way of thinking as important to hope.

CHRIST AS A NEW SELF

The issue of the relationship between God and the concrete
possibility, Christ, will become clearer if we state more precisely what the figure of Christ does. In its actual function,
this figure is the possibility of a new self. Christ makes concrete the new self that stands before the person.

Being a self means having a relation to oneself. An important part of that relation is the vision of an ideal self. For a
self that is growing and open to the future, the ideal self will
serve to give direction to the growth. Often the ideal may be
one toward which no growth takes place. In this case, the
ideal self will still serve as a standard for self-judgment, and
may often be the focus of a heavy load of guilt.

The figure of Christ is experienced as standing beyond the
ideal self that is part of the self-relation. Partly this results
from the way in which the figure transcends complete
embodiment. But there are other aspects of this figure which
define the specific kind of new self which is given and claimed
by Christ. To state them requires some choice of standpoint in
the great variety of the Christian tradition. Nevertheless, we
find three features which are essential to the figure of Christ
and which help to make clear why it cannot be experienced
simply as an ideal self. First, the new self with which the
figure of Christ confronts one is also a new world. That is, the
new self cannot be actualized in isolation. Second, the figure
of Christ points toward meeting with concrete existences as
the relationship through which the new self will be real.
Third, the figure of Christ breaks through the deficiency-
oriented striving toward an ideal self, and presents the new
self as a gift.

With regard to the first point, the interaction between new

self and new world, it is clear that the Christian faith has always had to struggle with a tendency to cancel out this interactiveness. As early as some of the opponents with whom Paul battled, there have been Christians who did not see the tie between new self and new world. The tendency has been the more compelling because the style of engagement with the world which is coherent with Christ rules out some of the most obvious ways of helping to make the new world actual.

In the second place, the figure of Christ is paradigmatic of a grappling with existence through the concrete other. The new self cannot be in its new world except as it finds and opens itself to other selves in a love that is free of the need to project one's own egocentric striving into the relationship. Thus the encounter is open to the actual, concrete other.

Thirdly, the new self is known as gift rather than as goal achieved. This is the central reason why Christ as new self stands beyond the ideal self so familiar to the self-relation. And this is the central reason why, after all recognition of the cultural-social functioning of this symbol of a new self, it is necessary to say that the figure of Christ brings to men a revelation of God. This is not to say that the figure of Christ works independently of a historical situation. Unless some person or social group expresses the acceptance of one's self, and provides a situation within which one can find a new possibility of selfhood supported and "given" in a social situation, it will be an exceptional person who will experience the new self as a gift. We clearly recognize that the element of gift as well as the element of claim in the figure of Christ is in large measure a function of the particular situation within which this concrete possibility comes to be known. But if we believe that historical-social situations are not to be understood in a causal-deterministic fashion, but are constantly open to the lure of God as they are reaffirmed by the actual occasions which make them up, then the figure of Christ will be not just a confirmation of social standards and social support, but a profound paradigm of a universal reality.

CHRIST AS A CHANGING FIGURE

The figure of Christ is remembered from the past, but the past does not fix this symbol in an immutable form. Christ is what we may call a "historical proposition." There is no timeless formulation of this figure, like the score of a symphony. No one expression is fully normative, not even the expression once realized in Jesus nor the Christ of the New Testament. Again, there is a parallel to other aesthetic objects. Homer cannot present the same form to us that his poetry did in the heroic age of Greece, and we cannot see in Dante what a thirteenth-century Florentine did. In the same way, the Christ of a nineteenth-century Russian monk is immensely different from what Christ means in an urban American church, black or white, and both are in many ways quite different from the forms of Christ known to early Christians. We have sketched in the previous section several characteristics of the figure of Christ which are both widely experienced and close to the center of Christ's meaning. Can anything more be said about the coherence of the figure of Christ in time?

The church has found three ways of meeting this question; each is still an important part of any answer. The first response of the church to the threat of the dissolution of the Christ-figure through historical change has been to establish the original expression as normative. The Scriptural canon became, so to speak, the score of the symphony. To this essential ingredient of an answer we shall return in a later section of this chapter on Jesus. But it is clear that the Scriptures do not function unequivocally as a norm to fix the figure of Christ. They express many other things besides this figure, and a perennial problem for the interpretation of the Bible is to find what is central in it. Besides, a stance of faith which is oriented to the future cannot be content merely with a norm from the past, even if that norm could be determined carefully. The first response of turning to the original expression is of particular importance in our own time, because it is a time that is discontented with the existing, current interpretations of Christ. Time and again the motif of return to the original figure has been a path to the recovery of power. The formally conservative stance of returning to the original Christ has often been functionally quite open to the future, partly because of the intrinsic power of the figure of Christ and the openness to the future implied in it, and partly because the very effort to return to the original faith meant a sharp break with the rigidities of the present, which opened the way for the new.

The second response of the church has been to recognize that the present experience of any time has to be taken as seriously as the figure in the book, if Christ is to be a vital figure, a symbol that can claim a full response. The embodiment of Christ in actual persons at a particular time is always the primary expression, however important the Scriptures are as a norm. To recognize the *important* present experience, however, is always difficult. Especially now, expressions of Christ outside the established ecclesiastical tradition often have both more power and more authenticity as representations of Christ than do the "authorized" interpretations. Passages from Dostoevsky or Bernanos, Faulkner or Salinger, or from rock music, often function as the symbolic vision that calls the figure of Christ to expression, more powerfully for many people than the New Testament.

To bring the present and the past together, the church has recognized the importance of development. Important here is the work of Newman, who developed the thesis that the new is the unfolding of what was implicit before. But in Newman's view nothing old ever disappears; the new is viewed in terms of its enrichment of the old. His was an immensely valuable insight, but not radical enough. Full recognition of the present has to be able to allow elements of the old vision of Christ really to be superseded and abandoned.

The third path taken to wrestle with the historical vicissitudes of the figure of Christ has been to see Christ as the figure toward which existence is tending, to see him as eschatological. Most of the time in Christian history this has been a subsidiary motif in the struggle with historical change. The reasons for this lie in the tendency, prevalent up to now, for a future orientation to function only in times of extreme crisis. A major task of a process Christology will be to rethink the eschatological meaning of Christ, Christ as the end, in terms that are meaningful not solely in a crisis situation.

The lines of this development can follow the lines of interpretation of the "end" suggested above in Chapter V. That is, Christ does not stand for a predetermined form of human existence, but stands for a selfhood that is fully open to the momentary encounter with the concrete beings which that existence encounters, in the faith both that such momentary but concrete encounters are of ultimate significance, and that the effort and hope, as well as the receptivity and "realization" which such encounters embody, are not merely of the moment but are taken up into God's recognition and enjoyment of reality.

An Example of Change

We may cite one example, taken from the sphere of the impact of the figure of Christ rather than directly from our grasp of the figure itself. Life in death is the central metaphor which this figure expresses. The discovery of a new self takes place through the loss of the old, and the loss of the old is not merely loss. It is loss *for* something; thus death and loyalty are interwoven. Traditionally we have interpreted this aspect of our appropriation of the central Christian symbol in terms of "What would you be willing to die for?" Such an interpretation of new selfhood through loss of the old is by no means exclusively Christian. It has been an almost universal test of self-transcendence, a use of the symbol of death that outreaches the particular symbol of the cross but certainly embraces one meaning of this symbol to Christians. Not long ago I was in a discussion with some young artists and actors, and one of them made the striking remark, "We must learn not to believe anything enough to die for it." How is one to interpret such a shift of a central component of what Christians have always found in Christ, an "obedience unto death"? The historian Andrew Hacker, quoted in *Newsweek* magazine for July 6, 1970, understands this shift, which he sees as a widespread one among young people, as a failure of loyalty, as a kind of withdrawal from responsibility. Like any new form of life, this one is still fluid and may take more than one direction. But I read it very differently from Hacker, as a reach toward a more universal loyalty rather than a failure of loyalty. The remark "We must learn not to believe anything enough to die for it" is a protest against the exploitation of loyalty by ideology; it is a call for a more universal vision. It is not too much to say that we see here a groping for a new manifestation of Christ.

It is not a spirit of imperialism which impels one to say that such efforts to discover a new life-style in which loyalty will not be so readily subject to exploitation will have the best prospect of success if they can find an explicit connection with the figure of Christ. The opposite course would be to say that the central metaphor of finding life through losing it is now appropriate to the figure of Christ itself, that is, that the time has come when the effectiveness of this symbol is becoming so diffuse that the centered form is no longer important. Christ may now lose himself in the general movement toward personal integrity and freedom. But if anything can keep these intimations of a more universal loyalty open, it will be contact with the deepest expressions of such questing in the past.

We may hope to see a new form of loyalty and sensitivity, less naïve about willingness to die for what one believes, and less tribal and exclusive, and we believe that this new style of loyalty will rightly be seen as responding to the figure of Christ, a Christ who will be seen as himself more flexible and adventurous than the traditional Christ. We take a clue from a remark of Amos N. Wilder, who comments about contemporary poetry that it is characterized by emphasis on the concrete and by improvisation or adventure, rather than by formal neatness of achieved structure.[3] These aspects of poetic language can point toward the new style of life which can be identified with Christ. The affinity between Christ and the concrete or definite has already been noticed. The note of improvisation and adventure points us to a universe that is open, within the flexible limits of its patterning, and toward a historical or processive order, in which the nodal points of meaning are concrete existences. Such a vision is coherent both with the groping for a universal loyalty expressed in the phrase "We must learn not to believe anything enough to die for it" and also with the gift and demand of a new self which Christians have always found to confront them in the figure of Christ.

The figure of Christ is still central in this changing style of existence, because it provides the focus by which one can find a ground for taking concrete existence, both one's own and that of the other, seriously. Despite the grotesque exaggeration of ego-consciousness in our culture, we cannot return to the ecstatic loss of the boundaries of the self as a fundamental way into the future.

CHRIST AS A LOCUS OF DEFINITENESS

It will help us to understand the kind of unification of experience that we find the figure of Christ providing if we observe that Christian thought has been struggling with this same problem for a long time, in different terms. Here again we confront the antithesis between the future as an anticipated definite but momentary unification of reality, and the future as the undifferentiated infinite that unifies by receiving all into itself. Though not cast in these terms, and usually not much concerned with God as *future*, the doctrine of the Trinity was wrestling with just this contrast. That is, the figure of Christ served to focus mystery in the definite and concrete rather than in the indefinite toward which it tends to turn if apprehended through the figure of God alone. This point was driven home to me in reading Jonathan Edwards, where the passionate sense of mystery is in tension between the infinite (symbolized by the sovereignty of God already discussed), before which finite reality is nothing, and the definite, symbolized by Christ who is not only a definite figure himself but also enables definite human existences to know themselves to have meaning despite the threat of God's sovereignty. Perry Miller's insightful book on Edwards clearly sees the way in which Edwards is grasped by the unfathomable mystery beyond the world, and he sets this sense of mystery in relation to later developments in the American imagination.[4] But though Miller sees the importance of definite existence for Edwards, as in his discussion of the story of the conversion of four-year-old Phoebe in the *Narrative of Surprising Conversions,* he does not see the importance for Edwards of Christ as opening the way to the definite as a focus of mystery. Conrad Cherry's interpretation of Edwards, in some ways not so innovative as Miller's, is much more adequate on this central point.[5] Cherry clearly shows how decisive the figure of Christ is to Edwards' vision, and how Christ shapes the architecture of his imagination to allow the definite focus not only of Christ himself but also of human persons to be the bearers of mystery.

Thus the infinite God and the definite Christ both serve as openings to mystery, neither isolated from the world, but both in closest interaction with it. If one's whole attention focuses on the infinite mystery of God alone, man would be reduced to nothing, or at least to a being who despises himself—a tendency clear enough in the style of thought we choose as our example, in the Calvinist's preoccupation with his own possible damnation. Edwards himself provides an important part of the background of the modern self-despising of man in his "Resolutions": "Resolved: that I will act so, in every respect, as I think I shall wish I had done, if I should at last be damned." [6] It is by virtue of the concrete and definite vehicle of wonder, Christ, that man is able to accept himself and take himself seriously, and also to see the wonder and mystery in the definite foci of reality about him. Christ prevents the escape into generality and ultimately into the undifferentiated infinite that is the other basic alternative to the soul that is seriously grasped by wonder.

With the definite we parallel hope; with the undifferentiated infinite, tranquillity. These are the two basic stances of faith, aside from the transitional stance of despair which has an unavoidable role to play in any life of faith but which can be only a transitional stance. The stance of tranquillity has an immense appeal today. It has its own integrity, and the style of Christian faith we envision will be far more open, ready to listen, and ready to learn from this alternative view than Christian faith has usually been. But in the last analysis Christian faith is a faith of definiteness and hope. Tranquillity has its role to play, but the self active in hope is its central gift. In religions of the Eastern type, it is the other way about; hope is a passing, perhaps youthful phase, and tranquillity is the ultimate wisdom. The difference lies in the effective functioning of the figure of Christ, through which one realizes the wonder of the actual other as of meaning not only in one's momentary realization of his existence, but also to God. Thus the formally unorthodox Christology suggested here is functionally incarnational or Trinitarian; it is an attempt to see in process terms how the infinite God deals with and comes to expression in finite and human reality.

CHRIST AS A LIVING FIGURE

The description of Christ so far attempted has not tried to account for the way in which Christ is experienced as a living reality. First, it should be seen that it is not only Christ who is experienced this way. To take an example which may not strike the reader as serious, but which is nonetheless illuminating, the most obviously fictitious literary figures are far more "living" than many really living people whom we know. The simplification of the self required by literary presentation does not necessarily reduce such figures to abstractions, but if skillfully done, suggests the depths and spontaneity that we find in actually living persons. We must start by recognizing that the corporate creativity of the church has presented such a "literarily" living figure to our experience.

In part we experience such a figure as living by virtue of a projection of our own living vitality into the symbol. If it is clear that this takes place in the case of the Christ figures in literature who mediate the figure of Christ to many modern people, why should it not be true of the figure of Christ himself?

Yet the figure of Christ is so persistently and profoundly experienced as having its own, and not just a reflected vitality, that we cannot accept the combined projection of the author's and reader's vitality into the literary figure as a complete model for understanding the living quality of the figure of Christ. This figure stands beyond and against the vitality of the person whom it confronts too sharply for this to be a total explanation. There are two possible further steps: either the inner vitality of the figure of Christ springs from its own independent life, or it is received from without. If the vitality comes from within, one can take the line of identifying a class of entities without bodily existence but with the power of interacting with human selves (angels or spirits). Such beings could find a place within a process system. Or this interpretation can take the course of supposing that Christ is the only entity of this sort. This view would normally include the supposition that the reality of Christ is a continuation of the series of personally ordered occasions that was Jesus. While others, we hope, will explore these avenues, it is clear from what was set forth in the chapter on eternal life that neither of these possibilities is followed here. In that chapter we showed that it is not clearly useful to suppose that surviving souls continue to interact with souls in bodies. It does not seem right to make Jesus an exception to this decision; to do so would make him remote from human existence. The view that "Christ" is a uniquely living reality though not a successor to Jesus, while it can be entertained theoretically, has nothing to commend it.

If Christ is experienced as a living reality in a depth that requires us to see a force at work here beyond the individual and social projection of our own vitality into the figure, and yet there is no sufficient reason to attribute an independent living quality to the figure of Christ, this vitality must be received from without. Then the symbol or proposition communicates the living reality of God himself. The symbol of Christ has a fundamental relation to Jesus, as we shall see below. But Christ is experienced as a living reality because this proposition or symbol serves, in the human situation, with decisive effectiveness to bring to awareness the living reality of God himself. It is because God is a living God, and made known as such through the figure of Christ, that Christ is experienced as a living reality.

We assume that the relation through Christ between God and the concrescing occasion of human experience arises from God's giving that occasion its initial aim in the form of a proposition. In human culture, propositions are always culturally mediated, but this is not an exhaustive description of them. In particular, the figure of Christ, by virtue of its combination of intense claim, beyond the capacity of men fully to embody it, with the gift of acceptance and the future as new life, cannot be exhaustively understood as a sociocultural product. The figure not only points beyond itself in the sense that it requires God if it is not to be irrational (as many modern thinkers, who reject the claims expressed in the figure of Christ because they reject the reality of God, have seen), but this figure also actually makes felt the living, personal, and loving reality of God. God reveals himself in Christ, in a decisively focused way.

CHRIST AND JESUS

The reality we know today as Christ functions rather diffusely in society. It can be thought that the movement of diffusion is both irreversible and good: that the death of Jesus is now being followed by the death of Christ, and that the former gives the clue to the interpretation of the latter—by losing itself in the wider movements toward creativity and life, the force at work in the figure of Christ will become more effective in the world.

We accept the view that the historically concrete symbol "Christ" will eventually disappear. We hope that this eventual disappearance may have the positive meaning suggested in the previous paragraph. What is correct in the above view is that God's purpose transcends what can be expressed in the one symbol "Christ" and that insofar as it is an expression of God's persuasion, the figure of Christ will lay men open to the task of bringing together the insights and purposes they derive from this symbol with others. We take this to be an instance of definite change in Christ, that while most earlier encounters with this figure found an exclusiveness in Christ which insisted that Christ is the center of all meaning, Christ does not today impart the claim to be a universal logos that excludes all meaning which cannot be derived from it.

Nonetheless, the notion that the disappearance of the figure of Christ into a generality of positive symbolizations is a hopeful process in our present situation is directly contrary to our reading of the situation. The reason is plain enough: the Christian style of existence is one that points to the inexpressible wonder and value of the concrete and definite. But the definite, whether the definite "other" who encounters us or the definite in our experience of the world generally, cannot remain a focus of meaning unless it can be related to some wider framework of meaning. We stand at a time of transition when established frameworks are changing or disappearing, and it is not the intention of this book to try to stop that process. But our judgment is that new thinking and new programs of practical action in the world have the best prospect of really taking account of the definite and concrete "other" as a focus of wonder and value if they respond to the future in the way we have sketched above as the response to the figure of Christ.

What has given a tough persistence to the definiteness and concreteness of the figure of Christ has been its association with Jesus. We know today that earlier Christians have often been naïve in identifying the two figures too completely. To work out fully how the figure of Christ is grounded in the historical Jesus is a task which reaches far beyond the scope of this study. It is clear that the power we find centering in the figure of Christ is by no means limited to Jesus and memories connected with him. Jesus was nonetheless the center of the storm which changed human consciousness so that the figure of Christ could be a concrete possibility for men. What the Christian believer sees in Jesus was also going on, usually in a less sharply focused way, around him as well. It should be clear from the earlier chapters that anyone who is trying to perceive what Christian existence is will have much to learn from those who probe the meaning of Jewish existence. But we still believe that there is a clear connection between Christ and Jesus. Two traditional ways of accounting for it are both still valid: one of them finds a focus of concreteness in the death of Jesus which rescues the figure of Christ from mythical generality, and the other looks back to the preaching of Jesus to find the beginnings of the style of existence which the figure of Christ lures men to actualize.

It is not possible here to work out either of these connections between Jesus and the figure of Christ. The first, which makes all the weight of definiteness and humanness rest in the bare fact that Jesus died, has been powerfully expressed by Rudolf Bultmann.[7] Some of his students have seen the importance of joining this emphasis with the second path which looks also into the memories of Jesus' message to find a basis for Christian existence.[8] My own point of view agrees with theirs. There is a real connection between the message of Jesus and the three points chosen above as central to the new self which the figure of Christ calls men to actualize: the new self is not private, but both brings and calls for a new world; the new self is real through grappling with existence in encounter with the concrete other; the new self is known as gift. Not only is this the case, but the Gospels and the New Testament generally are paradigmatic of Christian existence. That is, they open the meaning of the Christian style of existence to us in a way that touches the depths of our existence; they disclose the shape of this possibility with an intensity which, one can only say, we do not find matched in later accounts. The return to Jesus as the focus of concreteness is not merely a return to the past, but because of the clarity, depth, and passion with which the early records—and, behind them, Jesus— grasped the issues of what was then a new style of existence, this point of origin is of perennial value in reshaping our vision and orienting us to the future.

CHRIST AS NEWNESS AND HOPE

The figure of Christ was once a concrete focus of immense hope. Recent and extremely diverse New Testament studies have shown how strongly the Christ of the New Testament opened men's lives to a new freedom and a new future. In its first beginnings, this figure performed par excellence the kind of deformation of vision which remade the world of those who responded to it. Can Christ still function in this way, as a figure pointing and leading to the future? Despite what may seem to some an unnecessarily meager intellectual framework for interpreting the meaning of Christ, and despite the fact that this symbol is undoubtedly involved in a process of erosion, I am one of those who are profoundly gripped by the conviction that the figure of Christ is still the central focus of hope. That the power of this figure is diffused through the culture instead of functioning clearly through a recognizable social institution, and that Christ is a changing figure, has always been true, even though these facts are preeminently true today. We cannot meet these facts by returning to the older attempt at an ecclesiastical monopoly of Christ. But neither can we meet the difficult and fateful task of making true human encounter and true self-discovery possible today by blurring the distinctions between various good things. The hope that springs from the presence of the figure of Christ will be different from the original Christian hope, because it will know that it cannot expect a total resolution at the end. But it will also be like that original hope, because it will find its sense of wonder directed by trust, trust in the God of loving persuasion who has always been one of the central meanings that Christians have seen in Christ. And it will be like the hope of the first Christians in its paradoxical affirmation of life through death and of the inexpressible importance of the definite "other," for all his transience. Christ as the lure to actualization of the new existence will still claim the imaginations of men for living in the real world with hope and make them able not to despair at all that threatens and erodes the tenderness which is at the heart of hope.

Christ is still a potent figure, precisely at the central point of the modern struggle for life, the erosion of the self. The rebellion against the absolute God is the correlative of a rebellion against the heightened self-consciousness which that God provoked. To be rid of the assertiveness and guilt and the desire for domination which have been so stimulated in the modern thrust to break all boundaries—this is the hope which animates so many of the sensitive spirits of our time. This can be done by losing oneself in the indefinite infinite. But this means the sacrifice of the vision of historical existence which, in however debased a form, still shows its power throughout the world. For historical existence, existence in which men take responsibility for their mutual life and for their relation to nature, to be human, the forces focused in the figure of Christ must be powerful. The double function of fixing attention squarely on the concrete person here and now while opening the self to the persuasive power of God's purpose is still the function of Christ. The attempts to "move beyond" him turn out to be moves back to the nonhistorical, archaic style of existence.

In Retrospect, as We Conclude

Hope is the spirit in which we move into a future that we find genuinely open. By its trust in the future, hope makes love more than a momentary encounter; it makes us able to believe in the future of the one we love. Trusting the future in hope means that somehow the future takes us seriously, and takes those we love seriously. In other words, hope does not make sense unless there is some ground or basis of trustworthiness in life.

At the same time, the hope we experience exists in tension with despair. There is so much both within ourselves and in the world we know that is the opposite of hopeful. We must reach beyond ourselves if we are to hope. Yet the reach of traditional faith to a supernatural beyond easily makes hope escapist for those who find it possible, and is impossible for most modern men. Many honest spirits conclude that it is better to live in the world without hope, and others limit their hope strictly to what they can expect of human society.

If hope is to be valid and honest, it must take account of the harsh realities both of our own self-knowledge and of our public experience. It is possible to do this and still hope! The whole effort of this book has been to sketch a way of restructuring our imagination so that we can both be modern men and hope.

To renew our grasp of hope, this book has drawn both on the powerful vision of Alfred North Whitehead's process philosophy and on central insights of the Christian tradition. In spite of very real differences, Whitehead's philosophy of process as movement toward the future has much in common with the traditional Christian conviction that faith is expecting the end; both take time seriously and can lay us open to the future. We found that these two ways of thinking can illuminate each other.

Process philosophy offers a perspective on the world that is not man-centered, and yet takes value, beauty, and the future seriously. It has enabled us to see how hope has deep biological roots and is implied by man's restless creativity; and perhaps most important of all, process thought has provided a way of understanding the infinity of God in which the infinite God does not swallow up the concrete and limited realities on which we focus our creative effort and our concern, but takes them seriously as they come into being and pass away. From the process perspective we were able then to interpret a series of central Christian concerns to show that God can still be the center of trustworthiness (a trustworthiness essential for hope), even though we must drastically rethink God's relation to the world and be ready to see wonder in the world as well as in God.

For a process theology of hope there is no final end, but the trust in the future which Christians express in the traditional hope for the end is taken seriously in such a theology, as is the bold Christian belief that men are called by God to participate in the fulfillment of his purpose. A new perspective on eternal life, a perspective that takes real eternal life seriously but, we believe, is not escapist, also emerged from the dialogue between process thought and Christian faith. Finally, we saw how the figure of Christ, which came into our life as a result of the career of Jesus, is still an authentic and open power, and not a key to faith which is oriented to the past. The figure of Christ is a genuine mediator between God and man, and calls man to fulfill himself beyond himself in the future.

Can such a vision of Christian hope, rooted in the centuries of Christian experience yet reshaped by a contemporary understanding of reality, lay hold of men's imaginations to give them direction in such a time as ours? On first look, a process theology of hope may seem too theoretical. But as we find our way into this manner of thinking and it grips our imagination, we will discover that it is a view of reality within which the hope and expectation of Christian faith find resonance and confirmation. As we become familiar with it and test it out, a process theology opens a perspective that is both honest and full of hope and that is a ground from which to engage in the practical and social action in which hope must express itself in our situation.

APPENDIX
A Note
on Whitehead's Terminology

Although this book makes the effort to explain Whitehead's terms step by step as they are brought in, beginning with the latter section of the first chapter, this appendix offers a brief introduction to Whitehead's vision of reality and to the special terminology which he developed to give an account of that vision. His special terms are difficult, and purposely so, for they are intended to force us to think differently about the things that we think we know, and to see them in a new aspect. This brief sketch explains those Whiteheadian terms which are used earlier in this book, and can also serve as an introduction to those aspects of his thought which are important for the discussion of hope. We do not attempt to examine the problems or controversial points in the interpretation of Whitehead, since there are other works where that is done, and many important insights of Whitehead are passed over, since they are not used in this book.[1]

Whitehead's philosophy is a process philosophy. That means that what is real is what happens or takes place; that is, events are real. But we commonly think that what takes place "happens to" something that is steadily "there" before and after what happens, although perhaps changed by the event. Whitehead challenges us to take a quite different view of an event. The event itself is the actuality, a droplet of reality. He calls these fundamental bits of reality "actual occasions." Perhaps the best way to make clear what an actual occasion is, is to emphasize that it is an experience. Experiences, not static things or static minds, are the fundamental entities of which reality consists. "Experience" here includes the receptive side of what we commonly mean by experience: each actual occasion experiences or feels the immediately preceding occasions that provide it its data. "Experience" here also includes the freedom and self-determination of our everyday experience, for Whitehead believes that all the fundamental units of reality share, to some degree, in freedom and self-determination. Of course, freedom is trivial in low-grade occasions, though Whitehead's view makes it possible to take into account, in the same philosophical system, both the indeterminacy which modern physics has discovered and human freedom.

Thus the fundamental realities, the actual occasions, exist only briefly, coming into being as they receive from now-completed occasions the data which largely determine what they will be, but enjoying a moment of independent self-determination as they actualize themselves. For the process of transition from past occasions to those coming into being, Whitehead uses the term "prehension." Each occasion "prehends" the past occasions relevant to it. This prehension, or grasping, can also be described as feeling: each entity as it comes to be feels the impact of what has preceded it and must take account of this impact. Thus energy is transmitted to sub-atomic occasions, and thus we respond to and take account of the successive occasions of our experience.

As we note in the latter part of Chapter I, this vision of reality as a flow of successive actual occasions, each receiving input from the past but to some degree indeterminate, makes possible a fresh synthesis of two sides of our everyday experience which in much modern thought have fallen sadly apart: what we call the subjective and the objective. If we think of reality as made up of enduring "things," it is hard to see what effect subjective experience, thinking, feeling, and freedom can have in the world of things moved by things. If we construct a world out of subjective sensitivity or even of decision, it is hard to take the commonsense "objective" world as seriously as we actually have to do. We cannot here analyze Whitehead's careful account of how we know; he shows that even though our knowledge does arise from our experience, we do not have to be bound to a world of inner subjectivity but can attain real knowledge of the world. For our purposes, the important point is that "subjective" and "objective" are alternating aspects of each actual occasion. They are not persisting, opposing realities as in some dualistic systems of thought, nor is one of them unreal. Each actual occasion becomes an objective reality, fixed and determinate and inescapably "there" to have an effect on what follows. As it is prehended or felt by succeeding occasions it will work as an efficient cause. But each actual occasion also has its moment of being there for itself, of subjective independence; our experience of subjective freedom is taken with the utmost seriousness by Whitehead, and is generalized by him into one of the fundamental properties of all actual occasions, even though for simple occasions the degree of freedom is very small.

The process of coming-to-be of an occasion Whitehead calls "concrescence." The term suggests the making of a unity out of diverse data, and that is just what an actual occasion does. The concrescence of an actual occasion is a discrete "bud" or "droplet" of time, just as we experience time in separate bits, when we stop to examine it. And the independence of each occasion is emphasized to the point where during the process of concrescence, once it has received its data, the actual occasion is completely "on its own," a wholly private experience. Once the concrescence is complete, and the varied data have been synthesized into a unified "satisfaction," the occasion becomes a public datum that will be prehended or felt by succeeding occasions.

It is evident that when Whitehead asks us to think of the basic realities as actual occasions rather than as continuing things, he is pointing to realities which we do not experience as such, even though the elements of his description are related to things that we do experience. At the same time, science has taught us that the familiar objects which we experience are not really ultimate, and the basic components of which these familiar objects are made up (systems of energy) are very similar to Whitehead's "actual occasions." Indeed, mathematics and physics were deeply pondered by Whitehead as he evolved his thought. Instead of following this way of thinking about actual occasions, however, it is more important to note that while all the terms for analyzing the actual occasion are drawn from human experience (where else, ultimately, can they come from?), Whitehead points out that our main philosophical traditions have looked, for their clues about reality, at a part of experience which cannot be immediate experience of reality: this secondary part of our experience is composed of clear sense impressions. Deceptively "immediate" as these seem to be, they are immensely complicated abstractions, projected upon the world by our way of perceiving. Our actual experience of the world comes in tiny pulses of feeling, mediated to the responding occasion by the nervous system. Remember, too, that Whitehead insists that everything which can be experienced is already past. The pulse of feeling from a completed occasion is prehended by a succeeding one. Clear sense perceptions, on the other hand, give themselves out to be contemporary with the world which they represent. This alone shows their indirectness as experience of reality. We cannot follow further Whitehead's careful analysis of these two modes of experience: the basic but largely unconscious mode of "causal efficacy," in which we experience what has just happened and is affecting us, and the mode of "presentational immediacy," in which we experience the world as "there" in the present by a process of abstraction and organization of the pulses of feeling that have reached us.

If reality is as resolutely pluralistic as Whitehead supposed, how does it happen that there are such large uniformities in what we find in the world: stones, gases, organisms, and people with consistent characteristics? Clearly the first answer is that most occasions become what they do become predominantly by inheriting the characteristics of those which have preceded them. But if this were all that there is to it, the other feature of what we find could not be explained: the emergency of novelty. For novelty does not emerge in a purely random or chaotic way; the new builds on the old. To explain this combination of repetition and novelty Whitehead introduced two categories not mentioned as yet: eternal objects and God.

The element of uniformity in experience has often been explained, in other philosophies, on the basis that the many similar things all correspond to some idea or ideal reality. All examples of green are manifestations of the idea of green, for example. Such a philosophy may easily make the eternal ideas the basic (because enduring) realities, and consider the separate bits of green as secondary and less real. Whitehead was deeply concerned to do justice to the truth in these idealistic philosophies, though for him the momentary occasion rather than the idea is what is actual. "Eternal objects," which are potentialities or possibilities of some definite way in which an actual occasion may form itself, play an important role in accounting for the fact that events do not occur in a purely random way, but show striking uniformities. Such uniformities are realizations of a particular eternal object or possibility.

For Whitehead, eternal objects do not have any power or existence on their own. They are manifested as qualities of actual occasions. Further, Whitehead was convinced that if an actual occasion, as it came to be, received (prehended) its possibilities only from those expressed by the immediately preceding occasions, the result would be a universe of sterile stability, with no possibility of something new occurring. The same possibilities would endlessly repeat.

Thus he was forced to conclude that there must be a universally present purposive reality which offered to each concrescing occasion an aim that would, if appropriate, include significantly new possibilities or eternal objects. This reality Whitehead calls God, though he affirms God not for reasons of religious feeling but in order to give a philosophical account of the world. God's "primordial nature" envisages and orders all the infinity of possibility, and God provides each actual occasion with its initial aim, though the occasion in its unique freedom of self-realization may depart from this as it establishes its own subjective aim. The interplay between massive inheritance from the past, the aim at novelty derived from God in accord with his valuation of the relevant possibilities, and the spontaneous decision of the actual occasion itself accounts for the balance of continuity and change which we actually find in the world.

God's primordial nature, considered as a complete valuation of eternal objects or ordering of possibilities, is timeless, but it is equally important to conceive God as meeting the same requirements for reality that he found required for other actual entities. This means that God, like actual occasions, is involved in time; both God and actual occasions are actual entities or entities in act. God not only *gives* to the world (giving each occasion the initial aim that will best enable it to realize its possibilities), but *receives* from the world, feeling the intensities of pattern that occur in the succeeding actual occasions, taking account of everything that takes place and preserving in his "consequent nature" (his "memory") all that is worth preserving. Thus there is a constant interchange of feeling ("prehension") between God and the world. God and the world each require the other to be what they are.

God is not divided into two "natures," his primordial nature and his consequent nature. These are rather two functions of one reality. It should be said, however, that the primordial nature of God is that aspect of God which was most strictly required by Whitehead's philosophic analysis. The consequent nature of God is not so close to being philosophically necessary; Whitehead's treatment of this theme (mainly in *Process and Reality*, pp. 523-533) shows also his profound religious feeling. One could hardly affirm that God takes the world seriously, even suffers with it, and preserves eternally in his consequent nature all that is worth preserving except on the basis of a conviction that religious sensitivity brings to light a kind of evidence that philosophy must take seriously. At the same time, the consequent nature of God is not required simply to take account of what can be known by religious sensitivity, but also to account for the way in which God, in setting the initial aim of an occasion, relates this aim not just to the abstract world of eternal objects but also to the actual past of that occasion.

The relation of God, whose existence is everlasting, to the succession of actual occasions raises important questions that we cannot examine in detail. We follow the view that understands God, on the analogy of the human person, as a personally ordered series of occasions (see below). The successive occasions of God's experience are successive unifications of all his prehensions or feelings of the world.

One further remark about Whitehead's God: God's power is the power of persuasion. He offers to each occasion the initial aim which is best under the circumstances, the aim which when expressed will represent the richest, most intense synthesis of feeling possible for that occasion and will also take account of its relevant future. But the occasion, in its process of conscrescence, establishes its own subjective aim which may be a modification of the one offered by God. God cannot force an occasion to adopt a certain aim. And, of course, both God and the occasion are limited by the situation, by the concrete data from the past, in the context of which the occasion occurs. This limitation of God's power, however, opens the way for a new appreciation of God as the lure and persuasion to the better and to the future. It also strongly emphasizes that each occasion is a self-creation, and makes clear how God and the actual occasions need each other.

It was far from Whitehead's purpose to suggest that God is interested only in men. His view of God is set apart from many traditional theologies by his insistence that God's purpose and concern extend to all reality, and this view results from his philosophical position that there is not a sharp line of

distinction between human and other reality. Human existence is only one way in which intense value and responsible
freedom may become real. God intends the expression of
many other styles of value and not just the human. And God
and actual occasions work together in producing what actually
comes to be. There is thus no one goal for process, but an unending series of achievements. This salutary challenge to our
human egocentricity is especially relevant to the new ways of
thinking about nature that are required if we are not to destroy it.

At the same time, Whitehead's philosophy is extremely suggestive for our understanding of human existence. Any philosophy that makes the concrete occasion the real must confront
the complex continuities which are a special characteristic of
human life, for continuing existence is certainly the way in
which we experience ourselves. We do not consciously experience the separate actual occasions that, on this view, make up
a life.

Of course there are much simpler continuities. Any grouping
of occasions in which the members of the group depend on
other members for a common inherited characteristic is a "society of occasions." A series of occasions that inherits characteristics down a line of successive occasions (only one of
which exists at a time) Whitehead calls an enduring object. In
such a series, each occasion substantially repeats the feelings
of its predecessor. Stable objects that we perceive are collec-
tions of such enduring objects; an atom would be an example
of an enduring object or else a relatively simple collection or
corpuscular society.

A human person is capable of immensely greater spontaneity than an atom! Yet both share the trait of inheriting through
a series of occasions. The complexity of human experience and
response is in large part a function of the complexity of the
physical organism. But Whitehead insists that the human self
cannot be understood just on the basis of an interacting psychophysical organism. There is in human (and much animal)
life a single center of control and spontaneity: the dominant

occasion or presiding occasion which receives experience through the nervous system and acts as the controlling center of the organism. In another term, the controlling center is the soul—though not a spiritual soul as distinct from a material body, for the dominant occasion shares the basic makeup of all actual occasions. The soul is a personally ordered series of actual occasions, inheriting feelings down a successive line of momentarily existing dominant occasions. But its character is not determined simply by inheritance step by step from one momentary occasion to another. In the soul or series of dominant occasions, memory plays a role, enabling the response in the present to be relevant not only to the immediate past, but to a rich range of experience more remote in time. Further, human experience centering in the soul or dominant occasion is of a complexity and richness, and has a capacity for contrast and intensity, which is otherwise, surely, extremely rare.[2]

The complexity of human experience and our ability to make use of our past experience are both closely related to man's development of language. Whitehead has important things to say about language and symbolization, but this phase of his thought cannot be set forth here. We can call attention only to one specific point, which appeared in our final chapter. Recall that "eternal objects" are pure potentials. They are possibilities, regardless of their actualization. A "proposition," on the other hand, is an "impure potential." It is a possibility that has been related to a hypothetical subject. Propositions in Whitehead's system are not just entities in human existence or in conscious thought, but also function in many unconscious ways. Every occasion, conscious or unconscious, has a "subjective aim," which guides its concrescence. The subjective aim is best interpreted as a propositional feeling, the prehension of a proposition.[3] The subject of this proposition is the occasion itself; the predicate is the complex of eternal objects that it regards as a possibility for itself, that make up its aim. We find this analysis of the subjective aim as proposition extremely suggestive in interpreting the way in which the figure of Christ makes its claim.

Notes

Chapter I. Sex

1. Richard L. Rubenstein, "Thomas Altizer's Apocalypse," in John B. Cobb, Jr. (ed.), *The Theology of Altizer: Critique and Response* (The Westminster Press, 1970), p. 133.

2. For instance, Erik H. Erickson, *Childhood and Society* (W. W. Norton & Company, Inc., 1950).

3. James Agee and Walker Evans, *Let Us Now Praise Famous Men* (Houghton Mifflin Company, 1941).

4. See Roland M. Frye, "The Teachings of Classical Puritanism on Conjugal Love," *Studies in the Renaissance*, Vol. II (1955), pp. 148-159.

5. As by Abraham H. Maslow, *Religions, Values, and Peak Experiences* (Ohio State University Press, 1964).

6. Denis de Rougemont, *Passion and Society*, tr. by Montgomery Belgion (London: Faber & Faber, Ltd., 1940).

7. Abraham H. Maslow, *Toward a Psychology of Being* (D. Van Nostrand Company, Inc., 1962).

8. Marghanita Laski, *Ecstasy: A Study of Some Secular and Religious Experiences* (Indiana University Press, 1961).

9. Ernst Bloch, *Das Prinzip Hoffnung*, 3 vols. (Frankfurt: Suhrkamp, 1959), Vol. I, Ch. I.

10. Sigmund Freud, *Totem and Taboo* (New Republic, Inc., 1931).

11. The fundamental work is Alfred North Whitehead, *Process and Reality: An Essay in Cosmology* (The Macmillan Company,

1929). Also basic for Whitehead's thought are *Science and the Modern World* (The Macmillan Company, 1926); *Religion in the Making* (The Macmillan Company, 1926); *Adventures of Ideas* (The Macmillan Company, 1933).

12. Thus, Hans Jonas, *The Phenomenon of Life: Toward a Philosophical Biology* (Harper & Row, Publishers, Inc., 1966), p. 96, holds that Whitehead's emphasis on the actual occasion as the unit of reality, by breaking life up into a series of moments, makes it impossible to deal seriously with the continuity of a living being's life and with death as the final term of its existence. As will appear, we recognize that Whitehead's system can be seen in this way, but it does not require this interpretation.

13. Alfred North Whitehead, *The Function of Reason* (Princeton University Press, 1929), p. 8.

14. The discussion here on evolution is indebted to Richard H. Overman, *Evolution and the Christian Doctrine of Creation: A Whiteheadian Interpretation* (The Westminster Press, 1967).

15. Whitehead, *Process and Reality*, p. 164.

16. Overman, *Evolution*, p. 210.

17. *Ibid.*, p. 211.

CHAPTER II. THE CREATIVE ACT

1. Gregor Sebba, "Das Kunstwerk als Kosmion," in *Politische Existenz*, Festschrift for Eric Voegelin (Munich: C. H. Beck, 1962), pp. 525-540.

2. William F. Lynch, *Christ and Apollo: Dimensions of the Literary Imagination* (Mentor Book, The New American Library of World Literature, Inc., 1963), Ch. II.

3. Norman O. Brown, *Love's Body* (Random House, Inc., 1966).

4. Thomas J. J. Altizer, *The Descent Into Hell: A Study of the Radical Reversal of the Christian Consciousness* (J. B. Lippincott Company, 1970), p. 31.

CHAPTER III. THE INFINITE

1. Quoted in Nathan A. Scott, Jr., "The Recent Journey Into the Zone of Zero: The Example of Beckett and His Despair of Literature," *The Centennial Review*, Vol. VI, p. 151; reprinted in *Craters of the Spirit* (Corpus Books, 1968), p. 165.

2. Samuel Beckett, *Watt* (Grove Press, 1959), pp. 74, 76.

3. Altizer, *The Descent Into Hell: A Study of the Radical Reversal of the Christian Consciousness.*

4. *Ibid.*, p. 201.

5. John Woolman, *Journal*, ed. by Thomas S. Kepler (The World Publishing Company, 1954), p. 220.

6. William A. Christian, *An Interpretation of Whitehead's Metaphysics* (Yale University Press, 1959), pp. 271-277, emphasizes the minimal amount of ordering in God's primordial envisagement of possibilities. John B. Cobb, Jr., *A Christian Natural Theology Based on the Thought of Alfred North Whitehead* (The Westminster Press, 1965), pp. 155-156, speaks of "an indefinite variety of orders."

7. Charles Hartshorne, *The Divine Relativity* (Yale University Press, 1948).

8. *Ibid.*, p. 84.

9. John T. Wilcox, "A Question from Physics for Certain Theists," *Journal of Religion*, Vol. XLI (1961), pp. 293-300; Lewis S. Ford, "Is Process Theism Compatible with Relativity Theory?" *Journal of Religion*, Vol. XLVIII (1968), pp. 124-138.

10. Hartshorne, *The Divine Relativity*, p. 153.

Chapter IV. Secularization

1. Leslie Dewart, *The Future of Belief* (Herder & Herder, Inc., 1966), pp. 194, 196.

2. Peter Berger, *The Sacred Canopy* (Doubleday & Company, Inc., 1967).

3. *Ibid.*, p. 107.

4. Pierre Teilhard de Chardin, *The Phenomenon of Man*, tr. by Bernard Wall (Harper Torchbook, 1961), p. 284.

5. Harvey Cox, *The Secular City*, rev. ed. (The Macmillan Company, 1966), Ch. I.

6. Mircea Eliade, *The Sacred and the Profane*, tr. by Willard R. Trask (Harper Torchbook, 1961), p. 213.

7. Arend Th. van Leeuwen, *Christianity in World History* (Charles Scribner's Sons, 1966).

8. *Ibid.*, p. 170.

9. Whitehead, *Process and Reality*, pp. 315 f.

10. Herbert Butterfield, *Christianity and History* (Charles Scribner's Sons, 1950), p. 95.

11. Altizer, *The Descent Into Hell*, pp. 152 f.

CHAPTER V. EXPECTING THE END

1. Amos N. Wilder, "The Rhetoric of Ancient and Modern Apocalyptic," *Interpretation*, Vol. XXV (1971), p. 444.

2. W. G. Kümmel, in Hans Lietzmann, *An die Korinther I-II*, 4th ed., revised by W. G. Kümmel (Handbuch zum Neuen Testament, Vol. IX) (Tübingen: J. C. B. Mohr, 1949), p. 194.

3. The *telos* ("end") occurs in I Cor. 15:24, cited above; *eschatos* ("last") as an adjective is frequent in phrases such as "the last things" or "the last days" or "day."

4. Rudolf Bultmann, "Man Between the Times in the New Testament," *Existence and Faith*, tr. by Schubert M. Ogden (Meridian Books, Inc., 1960), pp. 248-266.

5. Paul Volz, *Die Eschatologie der jüdischen Gemeinde* (Tübingen: J. C. B. Mohr, 1934), p. 136.

6. Amos N. Wilder, *Eschatology and Ethics in the Teaching of Jesus* (Harper & Row, Publishers, Inc., 1950), p. 24.

7. Volz, *op. cit.*, p. 143.

8. See Oscar Cullmann, *Christ and Time*, tr. by Floyd V. Filson, rev. ed. (The Westminster Press, 1964), pp. 158-159.

9. Gerhard von Rad, *Old Testament Theology*, tr. by D. M. G. Stalker (Harper & Row, Publishers, Inc., 1962-1965), Vol. II, pp. 301-308.

10. See, e.g., IV Ezra 4:33-40; 8:14-19; Rom., chs. 9 to 11.

11. Volz. *op. cit.*, pp. 8-9.

12. Northrop Frye, *Anatomy of Criticism* (Atheneum Publishers, 1966), p. 136.

13. See John B. Cobb, Jr., *The Structure of Christian Existence* (The Westminster Press, 1967); Jack Boozer and William A. Beardslee, *Faith to Act: An Essay on the Structure of Christian Existence* (Abingdon Press, 1967).

14. Paul Tillich, "Das Recht auf Hoffnung," in *Ernst Bloch zu ehren*, ed. by Siegfried Unseld (Frankfurt: Suhrkamp, 1965), p. 268.

15. Teilhard de Chardin, *The Phenomenon of Man*, Book IV.

16. Rudolf Bultmann, *The Presence of Eternity: History and Eschatology* (Harper & Row, Publishers, Inc., 1957), p. 155.

17. Whitehead, *Process and Reality*, p. 27.

18. John B. Cobb, Jr., *God and the World* (The Westminster Press, 1969), Ch. IV.

19. Cobb, *The Structure of Christian Existence*, Ch. XII.

20. Charles Hartshorne, *The Logic of Perfection and Other Essays in Neoclassical Metaphysics* (The Open Court Publishing Company, 1962), Ch. X.

CHAPTER VI. PARTICIPATING IN THE FUTURE

1. A thorough and balanced recent summary of the controversy about the traditional two-source hypothesis, strongly supporting the hypothesis of Q, can be found in Werner G. Kümmel, *Introduction to the New Testament*, tr. by A. J. Mattill, Jr. (Abingdon Press, 1966), especially pp. 50-61. Cf. also James M. Robinson, "LOGOI SOPHON: On the Gattung of Q," in James M. Robinson and Helmut Koester, *Trajectories Through Early Christianity* (Fortress Press, 1971), pp. 71-113.

2. The traditional view that Q was teaching supplementary to the passion kerygma is represented, e.g., by Martin Dibelius, *From Tradition to Gospel*, tr. by Bertram Lee Woolf (Charles Scribner's Sons, 1935), pp. 245-246. The view that Q represents a distinct style of Christian proclamation is presented by H. E. Tödt, *The Son of Man in the Synoptic Tradition*, tr. by Dorothea M. Barton (The Westminster Press, 1965), pp. 232-269; Kümmel, *op. cit.*, p. 56, gives qualified assent.

3. Tödt, *op. cit.*, pp. 247-250.

4. *Ibid.*, p. 273.

5. Cf. C. H. Dodd, *Parables of the Kingdom* (Charles Scribner's Sons, 1936), especially Ch. II. Of course there are also the parables of the Kingdom, which Dodd interpreted in a realized eschatology sense.

6. On the question of the place of the Golden Rule in the message of the Synoptic Gospels, and in ancient ethical teaching generally, see Albrecht Dihle, *Die goldene Regel* (Göttingen: Vandenhoeck & Ruprecht, 1962).

7. So Tödt, *op. cit.*, pp. 118-120, 274.

8. Cf. Tödt, *op. cit.*, pp. 55-60, 64-67.

9. In all the literature on what Paul meant by "apostle," this point is perhaps most clearly brought out by Anton Fridrichsen, "The Apostle and His Message," *Uppsala Universitets Aarsskrift* (1947), 3.

10. This will be true no matter which interpretation of the "Messianic secret" is followed in detail.

11. James M. Robinson, *The Problem of History in Mark* (London: SCM Press, Ltd., 1957), pp. 59-60.

12. See Ch. V, n. 1.

13. I have dealt with Paul from the point of view of man's participation in God's work in *Human Achievement and Divine Vocation in the Message of Paul* (London: SCM Press, Ltd., 1961).

CHAPTER VII. ETERNAL LIFE

1. Alan Harrington, *The Immortalist* (Avon Books, 1969).

2. Rudolf Bultmann, "The Historicity of Man and Faith," *Existence and Faith*, pp. 92-110.

3. Gabriel Marcel, *The Mystery of Being* (Henry Regnery Company, 1959), Ch. II, p. 153.

4. See Robert Daglish's introduction to Valentin P. Kataev, *The Grass of Oblivion* (McGraw-Hill Book Company, Inc.), 1970.

5. Ernst Bloch, "Karl Marx, Death, and the Apocalypse," *Man on His Own*, tr. by E. B. Ashton (Herder & Herder, Inc., 1970), pp. 31-72.

6. Nikos Kazantzakis, *The Saviors of God*, tr. by Kimon Friar (Simon & Schuster, Inc., 1960), p. 93.

7. Teilhard de Chardin, *The Phenomenon of Man*.

8. Jonas, *The Phenomenon of Life*, pp. 268, 274.

9. Alfred North Whitehead, "Immortality," *Essays in Science and Philosophy* (Philosophical Library, Inc., 1947), p. 89.

10. Whitehead's view of immortality in the memory of God has been impressively developed by Charles Hartshorne; cf. his "Time, Death, and Everlasting Life," *The Logic of Perfection and Other Essays*, pp. 245-262.

11. Charles Hartshorne, *A Natural Theology for Our Time* (The

Open Court Publishing Company, 1967), p. 108; Paul Tillich, *Systematic Theology*, 3 vols. (The University of Chicago Press, 1951-1963), Vol. II, pp. 68-69. For these references and thoughtful comment on the subject, I am indebted to correspondence with C. W. Christian.

12. Whitehead, *Process and Reality*, pp. 166-167.

13. Cobb, *A Christian Natural Theology*, pp. 63-70; "Whitehead's Philosophy and a Christian Doctrine of Man," *Journal of Bible and Religion*, Vol. XXXII (1964), pp. 209-220; *God and the World*, pp. 101-102.

14. For a sample, consider the music reportedly dictated to Rosemary Brown by Beethoven and others and reviewed by Irving Kolodin in the *Saturday Review* of October 31, 1970.

15. Teilhard de Chardin, *The Phenomenon of Man*, p. 272.

16. Whitehead, *Adventures of Ideas*, p. 267.

CHAPTER VIII. CHRIST AND JESUS

1. Whitehead, *Process and Reality*, p. 281.

2. My perception of the functions of propositions has been enriched by reading Donald W. Sherburne, *A Whiteheadian Aesthetic* (Yale University Press, 1961).

3. Amos N. Wilder, *The New Voice: Religion, Literature, Hermeneutics* (Herder & Herder, Inc., 1969), pp. 183-200.

4. Perry Miller, *Jonathan Edwards* (William Sloane, Associates, Inc., 1949).

5. Conrad Cherry, *The Theology of Jonathan Edwards: A Reappraisal* (Doubleday Anchor Book, 1966).

6. Jonathan Edwards, "Resolution No. 51," in *Representative Selections*, ed. by Clarence H. Faust and Thomas H. Johnson (Hill & Wang, Inc., 1962), p. 42.

7. Rudolf Bultmann, "The Historical Jesus and the Kerygmatic Christ," in C. E. Braaten and R. A. Harrisville (eds.), *The Historical Jesus and the Kerygmatic Christ* (Abingdon Press, 1964), pp. 15-42.

8. We have in mind particularly Ernst Käsemann and Ernst Fuchs. See Norman Perrin, *Rediscovering the Teaching of Jesus* (Harper & Row, Publishers, Inc., 1967), and the bibliography there.

APPENDIX: A NOTE ON WHITEHEAD'S TERMINOLOGY

1. Whitehead's most important works for those who approach him from the perspective of religious thought are listed in Ch. I, n. 11. Among the introductions to Whitehead's thought the following are all clear and important; each is, of course, far more detailed than this brief sketch: Donald W. Sherburne, *A Key to Whitehead's Process and Reality* (The Macmillan Company, 1966); Victor Lowe, *Understanding Whitehead* (The Johns Hopkins University Press, 1962), a key section of which is reprinted in the useful volume, *Process Philosophy and Christian Thought,* ed. by Delwin Brown, Ralph E. James, Jr., and Gene Reeves (The Bobbs-Merrill Company, Inc., 1971); Ivor Leclerc, *Whitehead's Metaphysics* (The Macmillan Company, 1958). The most thorough analysis is William A. Christian, *An Interpretation of Whitehead's Metaphysics.* As a foundation for his own work John B. Cobb, Jr., presents a clear and nontechnical interpretation of Whitehead's metaphysics in his *A Christian Natural Theology Based on the Thought of Alfred North Whitehead.*

2. For more detailed treatment, see Cobb, *A Christian Natural Theology,* Ch. II.

3. On the subjective aim as a propositional feeling, see Christian, *An Interpretation of Whitehead's Metaphysics,* pp. 315-318.